RECHTSTHEORIE

Begründet von

Karl Engisch, H. L. A. Hart, Hans Kelsen
Ulrich Klug, Sir Karl R. Popper

Herausgegeben von Werner Krawietz

Brusiin-SONDERHEFT

New Approaches and Ways of Legal Thinking Revised

The Otto Brusiin Lectures 1982 - 1997

Edited by

Aulis Aarnio and Werner Krawietz

in Cooperation with

Panu Minkkinen

28. Band 1997 Heft 2

Duncker & Humblot · Berlin

RECHTSTHEORIE

Zeitschrift für Logik, Methodenlehre, Normentheorie und Soziologie des Rechts

Begründet von
Karl Engisch, H. L. A. Hart, Hans Kelsen, Ulrich Klug
Sir Karl R. Popper

Herausgegeben von
Werner Krawietz

Redaktionsanschrift: Prof. DDr. Dr. h. c. mult. Werner Krawietz, Lehrstuhl für Rechtssoziologie, Rechts- und Sozialphilosophie, Universität Münster, Rechtswissenschaftliche Fakultät, Bispinghof 24/25, 48143 Münster.
e-mail: Werner.Krawietz@uni-muenster.de

Redaktionsstab: Assessor Andreas Schemann, Assessorin Dr. Petra Werner.

Die Zeitschrift erscheint viermal jährlich im Gesamtumfang von ca. 552 Seiten. Abonnementspreis jährl. DM 164,– / öS 1.197,– / sFr 145,– zzgl. Porto, für Studenten jährl. DM 131,20 / öS 958,– / sFr 117,– zzgl. Porto, Einzelheft DM 45,– / öS 329,– / sFr 41,50 zzgl. Porto.

Bestellungen können an jede Buchhandlung oder direkt an den Verlag gerichtet werden. Abbestellungen müssen 6 Wochen vor Jahresende erfolgen.

Verlag Duncker & Humblot GmbH, Carl-Heinrich-Becker-Weg 9, 12165 Berlin
Ruf: 0 30 / 79 00 06 - 0, Telefax: 0 30 / 79 00 06 31

Satz: Fotosatz Voigt, Berlin
Druck: Berliner Buchdruckerei Union GmbH, Berlin

ISSN 0034-1398
ISBN 3-428-09600-2

Die Deutsche Bibliothek – CIP-Einheitsaufnahme

New approaches and ways of legal thinking revised : the Otto Brusiin lectures 1982 - 1997 ; Brusiin-Sonderheft / ed. by Aulis Aarnio ... – Berlin : Duncker und Humblot, 1998
(Rechtstheorie ; Bd. 28, H. 2)
ISBN 3-428-09600-2

This volume is dedicated to
Mrs. Hilkka Brusiin

Table of Contents

Addresses of the Authors

Prof. Dr. Dr. h.c. *Aulis Aarnio*, University of Tampere, Research Institute for Social Sciences, P.O. Box 607, SF-33101 Tampere

Prof. Dr. Dr. h.c. mult. *Ernesto Garzón Valdéz*, Rolandstraße 56, D-53179 Bonn, EGV@compuserve.com

Prof. Dr. *Hermann Klenner*, Gubitzstraße 40, D-10409 Berlin

Prof. Dr. Dr. Dr. h.c. mult. *Werner Krawietz*, Westfälische Wilhelms-Universität Münster, Lehrstuhl für Rechtssoziologie, Rechts- und Sozialphilosophie, Bispinghof 24/25, D-48143 Münster, Werner.Krawietz@uni-muenster.de

Prof. Dr. *Neil MacCormick*, The University of Edinburgh, Centre for Criminology and the Social Philosophical Study of Law, Faculty of Law, Old College, South Bridge, GB-Edinburgh EH8 9YL, eucl06@srv0law.ed.ac.uk

Dr. *Panu Minkkinen,* University of Helsinki, Faculty of Law, P.O. Box 4, SF-00014 Helsinki, panu.minkkinen@helsinki.fi

Prof. Dr. *Agustín Squella,* Universidad de Valparaiso, Facultad de Ciencias Juridicas, Economicas y Sociales, Avda. Errazuriz 2190, Casilla 123-V, Valparaíso, Chile

Prof. Dr. *Carl Wellman,* Department of Philosophy, Box 1073, Washington University, St. Louis, Mo 63130, USA

RECHTSTHEORIE 28 (1997), S. 141 - 142
Duncker & Humblot, 12165 Berlin

INTRODUCTION

The Otto Brusiin Foundation was established in 1984 through Mrs. Hilkka Brusiin's donation. The goal and purpose of the Foundation is to promote the interest in legal theory in Finland, to encourage especially young scholars to develop and deepen their international contacts as well as to support the interdisciplinary cooperation in the philosophy of law and social philosophy.

One of the main activities in cooperation with The Finnish Association for Legal Philosophy, a national section of the IVR, has been to organize a series of lectures dedicated to Otto Brusiin, who was the father of modern legal philosophy in Finland and an inspiring example for the younger generations.

By the financial support of The Otto Brusiin Foundation, the Association had a chance to invite in years 1985 - 1994 altogether six eminent scholars of the field of legal philosophy to give a special lecture on a topic connected to Brusiin's own thinking.

One of the lecturers, Professor Hermann Klenner knew personally Otto Brusiin who took actively part in the activities of the IVR organization by being a member of the executive committee of the IVR in the beginning of the 1950s. Professor Werner Krawietz, for his part, has long spoken in favor of Brusiin's thought within the German legal theoretical audience. Professor Krawietz was also the very person who most strongly supported the republishing of some of Brusiin's central texts with an introduction written by Professor Urpo Kangas ("Der Mensch und sein Recht", 1990).

All the other lecturers are also aquainted with Brusiin's thinking, and they introduced in their lectures original and new ideas concerning the topics which were most important for Brusiin himself, and also for many of his pupils. Unfortunately, Professor Agustín Squella was prevented from giving his lecture in person due to his obligations as the vice-chancellor of his university (Valparaiso, Chile), but his text is in its full-length included in this volume.

The editors of this collection of lectures hope that the reader will not only get in touch with Otto Brusiin's line of thought but also a fresh view about the ever occurring problems of legal theory and legal and social philosophy.

The Otto Brusiin Foundation, The Finnish Association for Legal Philosophy as well as the editors want to present their most cordial appreciation to Professor Dr. Dr. Dr. h. c. mult. Werner Krawietz, to Professor Dr. h. c. Norbert Simon and to the Publishing House Duncker & Humblot for having these lectures published in this special edition.

Aulis Aarnio and *Panu Minkkinen*

RECHTSTHEORIE 28 (1997), S. 143 - 155
Duncker & Humblot, 12165 Berlin

JUDICIAL DISCRETION AND CONSTITUTIONAL LAW

By Carl Wellman, St. Louis

Some measure of Otto Brusiin's philosophical importance can be seen by glancing about at the distinguished audience here this evening, for he, more than anyone else, planted the germinal ideas that have flowered into the Finnish legal philosophy that flourishes in our time. As Professor Aulis Aarnio has written:

> "Quite on the eve of the Second World War, in 1938, there finally appeared a study which in several senses may be also considered the growth ground of present day Finnish legal theory. This work was Otto Brusiin's dissertation, 'The judge's discretion in absence of the norm'..., an original and penetrating examination of the foundations of legal thinking."[1]

What subject could be more appropriate for this occasion, then, than a philosophical examination of judicial discretion?

Although I shall address Brusiin's subject and make use of his valuable insights from time to time, philosophical integrity demands that I approach this subject in my own way. Otto Brusiin was a distinguished Finnish jurist; I am merely a moral philosopher and a citizen of the United States. I do not apologize for my defects. I merely wish to be honest with you and to explain why I shall begin my philosophical inquiry with a fragment of the history of the United States Constitution.

The Constitution, as proposed to the original thirteen states for their ratification, contained no bill of rights. Alexander Hamilton argued that any such bill of rights would be both unnecessary and dangerous. It would be unnecessary because the text of the Constitution already contained guarantees of the most important political rights of the citizen; it would be dangerous because any list of constitutional rights could be interpreted to empower the federal government to deny any of the inalienable natural rights omitted from that list. But these arguments did not convince those who were fearful of a strong federal government. For a time, it appeared that it would be impossible to obtain the nine ratifications required for the new Constitution to go into effect. Then a political compromise was worked out. Several states agreed to ratify the

---

1 *A. Aarnio*, Legal Point of View, Helsinki 1978, p. 11.

proposed Constitution on the understanding that a bill of rights would be added to it immediately.

Thus it was that one of the items on the agenda of the first session of the Congress of the United States was the adoption of a bill of rights, subsequently to be proposed to the states for their ratification as the first ten amendments. James Madison, in presenting one of these, said:

> "It has been objected also against a bill of rights, that, by enumerating particular exceptions to the grant of power, it would disparage those rights which were not placed in that enumeration; and that might follow by implication, that those rights which were not singled out, were intended to be assigned into the hands of the General Government, and were consequently insecure. This is one of the most plausible arguments I have ever heard urged against the admission of a bill of rights into this system; but, I conceive, that it may be guarded against."[2]

The Ninth Amendment was introduced to protect against this danger. In the form in which it was finally adopted, it reads "The enumeration in the Constitution, of certain rights, shall not be construed to deny or disparage others retained by the people".

How well has this amendment served its purpose of giving legal protection to fundamental human rights not specifically mentioned in the United States Constitution? Not at all well. Indeed, during almost two hundred years of legal history, the Ninth Amendment has been seriously considered in hardly a score of cases, and in only two has it made any important contribution to the decision of the court. Why this almost complete neglect of this potentially very powerful provision of the Constitution? The reason, I believe, is that it threatens almost unlimited judicial discretion. How is the court to apply the Ninth Amendment? Presumably by interpreting it to provide legal protection to some right retained by the people. But how is the court to identify those retained rights? Since these are not enumerated, not mentioned at all in the text of the Constitution, the Ninth Amendment seems to invite unlimited speculation. Suppose that some such right, say the right to interstate travel or the right to privacy, could be identified. How is its content to be defined precisely enough to determine whether it is or is not applicable to the case before the court? On these crucial, and controversial, questions, the law appears to be completely silent. It may be, as H. L. A. Hart has argued, that the open texture of language renders judicial discretion ineradicable from the law. It may even be, as many believe, that judicial discretion in small doses is desirable in order to render general legal norms flexible enough to apply usefully and justly to unanticipated developments. But in such large doses, judicial discretion threatens to

---

[2] *Griswold v. Connecticut*, 381 U.S. 479, p. 489.

destroy legal certainty and to render judicial decisions completely arbitrary and, therefore, unjust. Let us not forget that a medication as common and useful as aspirin can, when taken in excess, cause internal haemorrhaging and even death.

Has this judicial neglect of the Ninth Amendment been wise restraint of foolish timidity? Should we, as citizens, judges or philosophers of law, regard the judicial discretion permitted, even required, by any application of this amendment as a threat to the rule of law or an opportunity for constitutional change? To answer these questions, let us examine two of the opinions in the case of *Griswold v. Connecticut*, the case which first established the constitutional right to privacy in United States law.

The facts of the case are simple. Griswold, Executive Director of the Planned Parenthood League of Connecticut, and Buxton, a licensed physician who served as Medical Director for the League at its Centre in New Haven, were charged with giving information, instruction, and medical advice to married persons as to the means of preventing conception. The State of Connecticut had enacted a statute which made it a crime to use any drug, medicinal article or instrument for the purpose of preventing conception. Griswold and Buxton were found guilty in the Connecticut courts of being accessories to this crime of using contraceptive devices. They appealed their conviction to the Supreme Court of the United States alleging that the Connecticut statute was unconstitutional. Their argument was that it violated the right to privacy of married couples.

The obvious difficulty in their case lies in the fact that the United States Constitution nowhere mentions any right to privacy. Nevertheless, the Supreme Court found for the appellants on the ground that the right to privacy is one of those unenumerated rights protected by the Ninth Amendment. Justice Douglas, who delivered the opinion of the court, found the right to privacy in the penumbras of several of the rights, such as the right to freedom from unreasonable searches and seizures, in the Bill of Rights. Justice Harlan, in a concurring opinion, found it in the right to liberty protected by the Due Process Clause of the Fourteenth Amendment. In the concurring opinion most relevant to our concerns, however, Justice Goldberg found the right to privacy in the Ninth Amendment itself.

Goldberg argued that the language and history of the Ninth Amendment reveal that the framers of the Constitution believed that there are additional fundamental rights that exist alongside those specifically mentioned in the Bill of Rights and that those rights are intended to be protected by the Amendment from governmental infringement. To hold that a right so basic and fundamental as the right to privacy may be violated by the State of Connecticut would be to ignore the Ninth Amendment and to be unfaithful to the Constitution by giving one of its provisions no effect whatsoever. How did he know that the right to privacy is one of the rights retained by the people?

> "In determining which rights are fundamental, judges ... must look to the 'traditions and [collective] conscience of our people' to determine whether a principle is 'so rooted [there] ... as to be ranked as fundamental.' ... The inquiry is whether a right involved is of such a character that it cannot be denied without violating those 'fundamental principles of liberty and justice which lie at the base of all our civil and political institutions'..."[3]

He concluded, applying these tests, that the right to privacy is a fundamental right protected by the United States Constitution.

Would it be desirable for future courts to follow the example of Justice Goldberg by taking advantage of the judicial discretion offered by the Ninth Amendment to give legal recognition to additional fundamental rights not specifically mentioned in the Constitution? Justice Black, who severely criticized Goldberg's legal reasoning in a dissenting opinion, thinks not. I would favour increased use of this amendment. Let us see what can be said on both sides of this issue.

Why are constitutional rights important? What is the essential purpose of establishing constitutional rights in any legal system? Those who objected so strenuously to ratifying the Constitution as originally proposed believed that a bill of rights was necessary to give legal protection to the fundamental rights, that were then called natural rights and are today called human rights, of those subject to the law. But they also recognized that any bill of rights would be incomplete. Hence, the reason for having constitutional rights in the first place implies the need to give the courts discretion to recognize additional fundamental rights as they become threatened. Only thus can fundamental human rights be completely and adequately secured by any legal system.

Justice Black rejects this reasoning. Indeed, he insists that judicial discretion is incompatible with the essential purpose of constitutional rights. If the purpose of constitutional rights is to *protect* the fundamental rights of the individual against governmental infringement, then these rights must be written into the law in clear language that leaves no room for reinterpretation.

> "One of the most effective ways of diluting or expanding a constitutionally guaranteed right is to substitute for the crucial word or words of a constitutional guarantee another word or words, more or less flexible and more or less restricted in meaning. This fact is well illustrated by the use of the term 'right

---

3 *Griswold* (note 2), p. 493.

of privacy' as a comprehensive substitute for the Fourth Amendment's guarantee against 'unreasonable searches and seizures'. 'Privacy' is a broad, abstract and ambiguous concept, which can easily be shrunken in meaning but which can also, on the other hand, easily be interpreted as a constitutional ban against many things other than searches and seizures."[4]

He concludes that individual rights are securely protected only if the courts stick to the simple language of the Constitution.

I understand his concern. If judges have discretion to reinterpret the language of the Constitution in any way they please, in effect to rewrite the Constitution according to their whims, then constitutional law provides at best a fragile and insecure protection for human rights. On the other hand, his solution to this very real problem is entirely unworkable. Granted that privacy is "a broad, abstract and ambiguous" concept, so is the concept of "searches and seizures", not to mention the qualification "unreasonable". Is tapping my private telephone line without my permission an unconstitutional search of my home? If the police take information from my income tax return to try to implicate me in drug trafficking, is this a seizure? There is no way to escape the need for judicial interpretations of the language of the law, and even the clearest of language leaves some room for discretion in choosing between alternative interpretations. This is especially true of constitutional law, for constitutional documents are typically brief and formulated in the most general and abstract terms. If this fact escaped the notice of Justice Black, this is probably because the words "searches and seizures" have been given very concrete and precise meanings by centuries of judicial application. Far from undermining the security of fundamental rights, judicial interpretation secures their protection by translating the abstract and ambiguous language of the Constitution in ways that make it clear precisely what the government is not permitted or empowered to do to the individual citizen.

Another reason to take advantage of the judicial discretion offered by the Ninth Amendment is to introduce desirable changes into constitutional law. Legal certainty is no doubt a virtue, but legal rigidity is not. As Aarnio reminds us, "One of Brusiin's starting-points is the *dynamical* ... nature of legal thinking".[5] The need for legal change is imperative because law is an instrument of social regulation and social conditions are continually changing. Constitutional law tends to change more slowly than statute law; this is especially true in jurisdictions where there is a written constitution and in which this fundamental legal document cannot be changed by the normal legislative procedures. Where

---

4 *Griswold* (note 2), p. 509.

5 *Aarnio* (note 1), p. 13.

constitutional amendment is difficult, and consequently infrequent, judicial discretion serves the very valuable purpose of enabling the courts to reinterpret legal rules and principles so that they apply beneficially and justly to new situations.

It is not just the social situations to which the law is applied that change; the moral consciousness of any society changes also. Constitutional law quite properly reflects and serves moral ideals. As the community's moral insight changes, so should its law. A decade before the *Griswold* case, Bennet Patterson wrote an influential book in which he pleaded for the use of the Ninth Amendment as a means of moral reform.

> "We believe that the Ninth Amendment was intended to protect the unenumerated rights, not only as they have now appeared, but also as such rights may appear as history and the future shall unfold. As the race becomes more evolved, and as the respect for the dignity of human life increases; as we become more intelligent and spiritual human beings, then we shall learn more of the fundamental truths about human nature."[6]

An important reason to welcome judicial discretion is to facilitate legal change to adapt the constitution to changing social circumstances and achieve moral reform of an imperfect legal system.

As one might expect, Justice Black rejected this argument.

> "The idea is that the constitution must be changed from time to time and that this Court is charged with a duty to make those changes. For myself, I must with all deference reject that philosophy. The Constitution makers knew the need for change and provided for it. Amendments suggested by the people's elected representatives can be submitted to the people or their selected agents for ratification ... And so, I cannot rely on the Due Process Clause or the Ninth Amendment or any mysterious and uncertain natural law concept as a reason for striking down this state law."[7]

Black recognizes the need for constitutional change, but holds that it should be brought about by the process of formal amendment rather than judicial interpretation. Unfortunately, the amendment process in United States constitutional law is so cumbersome that the Constitution has been amended a mere twenty-six times in almost two centuries. This strongly suggests that this means of constitutional change is inadequate and needs to be supplemented with another, presumably the exercise of judicial discretion. However desirable it might be to have the United States Congress propose amendments and to have them ratified by the States, this simply will not happen often enough to eliminate the need for constitutional changes introduced by the courts. For this reason, if no

6 *B. B. Patterson,* The Forgotten Ninth Amendment, Indianapolis 1955, p. 52.
7 *Griswold* (note 2), p. 522.

other, I would welcome an increased use of the Ninth Amendment in judicial reasoning.

Justice Black resists this conclusion. It is not discretion as such to which he objects; it is *judicial* discretion, especially the sort of judicial discretion left by the Ninth Amendment, that he distrusts.

> "The adoption of such a loose, flexible, uncontrolled standard for holding laws unconstitutional, if ever it is finally achieved, will amount to a great unconstitutional shift of power to the courts which I believe and am constrained to say will be bad for the courts and worse for the country."[8]

It will be bad for the courts because they are ill-equipped to legislate. By training and long practice, judges are highly skilled at applying legal rules or principles to particular cases. But no court has enough judges to reflect the competing groups in any society so as to arrive at a law that can be expected to reflect the political views of the community. Indeed, judges are typically appointed rather than elected precisely to insulate them from the political process. Moreover, courts lack the committee system by which proposed laws can be subjected to extended debate and through which relevant information can be collected in order to arrive at wise legislation. It would be worse for the country because it would violate the separation of powers essential to the United States Constitution. The inevitable consequence will be excessive political power in the hands of a few judges, judges who are not subject to reelection and, therefore, who cannot be effectively held responsible for the exercise of their power.

Now I would agree that judicial discretion does confer power and that it would be most undesirable to confer uncontrolled power upon the courts. But this merely shifts attention to the first part of Black's argument. Would the use of the Ninth Amendment necessarily mean the adoption of "a loose, flexible, uncontrolled standard"? Here we confront the crucial issue dividing Black and Goldberg.

Justice Black insists, and I would agree with him, that judicial discretion is legitimate only where its exercise is subject to fixed standards and that it is impermissible for judges to impose their personal preferences upon the parties to any case before the court. He quotes Justice Iredell and Learned Hand to show that any judicial appeal to the Ninth Amendment is ruled out on these grounds.

> "The ideas of natural justice are regulated by no fixed standard: the ablest and the purest of men have differed upon the subject; and all that the Court could properly say, in such an event, would be, that the Legislature (possessed of an equal right of opinion) has passed an act which, in the opinion of the judges, was inconsistent with the abstract principles of natural justice.

---

[8] *Griswold* (note 2), p. 521.

Judges are seldom content merely to annul the particular solution before them; they do not, indeed they may not, say that taking all things into consideration, the legislator's solution is too strong for the judicial stomach. On the contrary they wrap up their veto in a protective veil of adjectives such as 'arbitrary', 'artificial', 'normal', 'reasonable', 'inherent', 'fundamental', or 'essential', whose office usually, though quite innocently, is to disguise what they are doing and impute it to a derivation far more impressive than their personal preferences, which are all that in fact lie behind the decision."[9]

Justice Goldberg, whose opinion is based squarely upon the Ninth Amendment, naturally denies these charges.

"In determining which rights are fundamental, judges are not left at large to decide cases in light of their personal and private notions. Rather, they must look to the 'traditions and [collective] conscience of our people' to determine whether a principle is 'so rooted [there] ... as to be ranked as fundamental.'" *Snyder v. Massachussetts,* 291 U.S. 97, 105. The inquiry is whether a right involved is of such a character that it cannot be denied without violating those 'fundamental principles of liberty and justice which lie at the base of all our civil and political institutions'..." *Powell v. Alabama,* 287 U.S. 45, 67.[10]

He defends his use of the Ninth Amendment by asserting that, although it may have left him considerable judicial discretion, his exercise of that discretion was subject to and in fact conformed to fixed standards established in earlier decisions of the Supreme Court.

Are the standards to which Goldberg subscribes the appropriate standards to govern the exercise of judicial discretion in this case? Well, this case hinges on an alleged unenumerated right, the right to privacy. Whether the tests used by Goldberg are the correct ones seems to depend upon what they are tests for – that is, upon the nature of those unenumerated rights retained by the people.

Presumably these were natural rights. Patterson points out that most of the members of the Constitutional Convention had previously signed the Declaration of Independence, which had affirmed:

"We hold these truths to be self-evident, that all men are created equal, that they are endowed by their Creator with certain unalienable Rights, that among these are Life, Liberty and the pursuit of Happiness. That to secure these rights, Governments are instituted among Men, deriving their just powers from the consent of the governed."[11]

Moreover, the political philosophy of Locke and the legal theory of Blackstone, implicit in this Declaration, were widely accepted by those who participated in the debates over the ratification of the Constitution

---

9 *Griswold* (note 2), pp. 525, 513.

10 *Griswold* (note 2), p. 493.

11 *Patterson* (note 6), p. 8.

and very probably motivated the insistence upon adding a bill of rights. The Ninth Amendment, then, was intended to protect the fundamental natural rights retained by the people when they entered into the social contract establishing the United States Constitution.

But if the unenumerated rights are Lockean natural rights, one would think that the appropriate test for the reality of any alleged right would be the light of reason or rational intuition. This is precisely why Justice Black rejects any and all natural law reasoning, for what is self-evidently true to one person is self-evidently false to another. Hence, to allow self-evidence into judicial reasoning is to abandon fixed standards and to admit uncertainty and controversy into the law.

Justice Goldberg, however, does not appeal to rational intuition. He does not assert merely that it is self-evident that there is a natural right to privacy. The tests that he uses are the traditions and conscience of our people and the principles of liberty and justice which lie at the base of all our civil and political institutions.

At first glance these tests seem more appropriate to institutional rights, what were called the traditional rights of Englishmen, than to natural rights, fundamental moral rights whose existence is supposed to be independent of public opinion and social institutions. As a moral philosopher, I would argue that our knowledge of human rights cannot come primarily from the application of Goldberg's tests. There must be some other, and independent, form of moral reasoning to establish the existence or nonexistence of any fundamental moral right. Precisely what that is is a difficult, and controversial, philosophical problem.

It does not follow, however, that Goldberg's tests are inappropriate. Even if the ultimate grounds of human rights must be found elsewhere, the traditions and conscience of our people and the principles of liberty and justice which lie at the base of our political institutions might still be *tests* for natural rights if there was any reason to believe that they were somehow associated with these ultimate grounds. Sir William Blackstone certainly believed in such a correlation.

> "The absolute rights of every Englishman (which, taken in a political and extensive sense, are usually called their liberties,) as they are founded on nature and reason, so they are coeval with our form of government; though subject at times to fluctuate and change; their establishment (excellent as it is) being still human."[12]

If one believes that the conscience of a people is reasonable and by and large correct, then one can justifiably believe that that conscience is a

---

12 *W. Blackstone,* Commentaries on the Laws of England, Book 1, Philadelphia 1902, p. 114.

test, not infallible but credible, of the existence of our natural rights. If one grants that the moral principles presupposed by our political institutions approximate to the truth, one might use as a test for the reality of some alleged moral right the principles found to be implicit in our institutions.

I will go even further. It seems to me quite appropriate for a legal system to establish a legal presumption in favour of any affirmed right that meets tests such as these. To be sure, these tests are at best derivative and at worst misleading. They presuppose the existence of some other prior method of establishing the existence of a human right and derive their validity from their imperfect correlation with this more basic form of moral reasoning. Admittedly, the application of these imperfect tests will sometimes lead the courts to morally unjustified conclusions. What I would maintain, however, is that even on those occasions, the judicial decisions will be legally, if not morally, justified. One might imagine that the courts ought to use the more basic forms of reasoning appropriate for moral philosophy, but this is not so. Typically, moral philosophers disagree much more often than they agree. In philosophy, this is more of an opportunity than a calamity, for it is from disagreement that new and fruitful philosophical investigations spring. In the law, this would be undesirable. An essential function, perhaps the primary purpose, of the courts is to settle disputes. For this purpose, judges must appeal to generally accepted and relatively undisputed premises in their reasoning. Hence, for the special purposes of the courts, a public test, such as the conscience of the people or the principles at the base of our public institutions, is more appropriate than the individual reasonings or moral insights of a philosopher, even a philosopher as wise and invariably correct as I.

There is a third, and most important, reason to consider the tests used by Justice Goldberg the appropriate ones to govern his exercise of judicial discretion in the Griswold case. He did not invent these tests or discover them on his own initiative. He established their legal authority by citing legal precedents, specifically *Snyder v. Massachussetts* for the first test and *Powell v. Alabama* for the second. It is my contention that the legally appropriate tests are those accepted as tests by the courts. Why this is so can be explained only after a consideration of the nature of constitutional law.

It is often asserted that while the United States Constitution is a written document, the Constitution of the United Kingdom consists entirely of legal practices. To my mind, neither claim rings true. No less an authority than A. V. Dicey informs us that the Constitution of the United Kingdom is not entirely unwritten.

"There are laws of the constitution, as, for example, the Bill of Rights, the Act of Settlement, the Habeas Corpus Acts, which are 'written law', found in the statute-books – in other words are statutory enactments. There are other most important laws of the constitution (several of which have already been mentioned) which are 'unwritten' laws, that is, not statutory enactments. Some further of the laws of the constitution, such, for example, as the law regulating the descent of the Crown, which were at one time unwritten or common law, have now become written or statute law."[13]

On the other hand, Stephen Munzer and James Nickel explain why it is incorrect to identify the constitutional law of the United States with any written document.

"Reflection reveals, however, that the clauses of the U. S. Constitution are, in at least two ways, only partial formulations of constitutional law. First, these clauses do not give the full or exact scope of all constitutional rules specified in the text; to determine that one must, among other things, read the relevant cases. Second, they do not even mention some constitutional rules, namely those which, like the right to travel and the right to privacy, are not found in any particular provision of the text."[14]

In short, no adequate account of the United States Constitution can ignore the practices of the courts.

They advocate, therefore, a conception of constitutional law that regards written documents and legal practices as inseparably related to one another.

"This Article ... presents our Constitution as a textbased institutional practice. It is thus opposed to theories, like the 'historical approach', which see the constitution simply as an original text together with an accretion of historically correct interpretations, and to theories, like Karl Llevellyn's, which see it as just a complicated institution."[15]

They are using the word "practice" in a very special sense best explained by John Rawls.

"I use the word 'practice' throughout as a sort of technical term meaning any form of activity specified by a system of rules which defines offices, roles, moves, penalties, defenses, and so on, and which gives the activity its structure. As examples one may think of games and rituals, trials and parliaments."[16]

It is no accident that trials and parliaments are paradigms of practices because the law consists of an interlocking set of social practices. Nor is it any accident that legal practices are text-based, for legal rules func-

---

[13] *A. V. Dicey,* Introduction to the Study of the Law of the Constitution, 10. edition, London 1959, p. 28.

[14] *S. R. Munzer / J. W. Nickel,* Does the Constitution Mean What It Always Meant? In: Columbia Law Review 1977, pp. 1042 - 1043.

[15] Ibid., pp. 1029 - 1030.

[16] *J. Rawls,* Two Concepts of Rules, in: Philosophical Review 1955, p. 3.

tion as social norms and, as G. H. von Wright has observed, "It is an essential feature of norms that they should be expressible in language, in what I propose to call normformulations".[17] I believe that this conception of a textbased practice fits both the United States Constitution and the Constitution of the United Kingdom.

Since constitutional law is a text-based practice, one legal theorist may focus upon the written text while another pays greater attention to legal practices. The former is apt to think of a legal system as a logically structured set of rules expressible, ideally, in some standard logical notation; the latter is more inclined to think of a legal system as an interlocking set of legal institutions, such as legislatures and courts, and to characterize the law in terms of the activities and functions of these institutions. Otto Brusiin recognized this when he wrote:

> "Some legal theorists concentrate especially on logical problems in the field of law, while others are mainly occupied with human behaviour in its relations to legal norms. Both aspects, logical and sociological, necessarily enter every legal theory."[18]

Which aspect is more basic or more important? It was his view, expressed in his own work, that the sociological aspect is primary because law is a thoroughly social matter.[19] I completely agree with Brusiin on this important point. Notice that I have adopted the view that constitutional law is a text-based practice, not a practice-modified text. What is central and essential to law is a set of legal practices, but because these are normative practices texts play a crucial role in them.

We are now in a position to understand why I contended, a moment ago, that the legally appropriate tests for the unenumerated rights are those accepted as such by the courts. The text of the United States Constitution includes not merely the original document together with all twenty-six amendments, but also all the opinions of federal judges based upon these. Thus, the tests used by Justice Goldberg to show that the right to privacy is one of the unenumerated rights protected by the Ninth Amendment are found in the text of the Constitution, for they are found in the judicial opinions he cites. But what gives these opinions their legal authority? Precisely what gives the original document its authority, the judicial practice of recognizing these texts as the highest law of the United States and applying them to cases before the federal courts. Moreover, it is this same judicial practice that protects our legal system from the dangers of excessive judicial discretion threatened by

---

17 *G. H. von Wright,* Is and Ought, in: E. Bulygin/J.-L. Gardies/I. Niiniluoto (eds.), Man, Law and Modern Forms of Life, Dordrecht 1985, p. 8.

18 *O. Brusiin,* Legal Theory, in: ARSP 1957, p. 467.

19 *Aarnio* (note 1), p. 13.

the Ninth Amendment. Just as a series of interpretations and applications of a statute formulated in very abstract and indeterminate language gradually renders that statute more unambiguous, determinate and precise, so the use of the Ninth Amendment by the courts would generate a series of legal precedents that would gradually reduce the range of judicial discretion it permits and provide increasingly definite standards for its interpretation.

Although appropriate and legally authoritative, the standards cited by Goldberg need not be the last word on the subject. They could, and perhaps should, be developed further by the ongoing practice of judicial interpretation as they are applied to new cases arising under changing circumstances. Since the natural rights of traditional political and legal theories, such as those of Locke and Blackstone presupposed by the Ninth Amendment, are today spoken and thought of as human rights documents, such as the United Nations Universal Declaration of Human Rights of 1948 and the much more recent Declaration of Helsinki, are partial evidence for the existence of a fundamental moral right retained by the people under the United States Constitution.

It is clear enough why I, a moral philosopher and a citizen of the United States, should wish to lecture on the Ninth Amendment. But why should you, Finnish philosophers of law listening to me here in Helsinki, be interested in my subject? It is, I believe, because this small part of the constitutional law of my country raises larger philosophical issues equally important in understanding every legal system, including your own. These include difficult problems concerning the desirability of judicial discretion and the standards that ought to govern its exercise. The danger of excessive, almost unlimited discretion, to which I have paid particular attention, arises in any legal system that permits natural law reasoning or allows moral norms to enter into judicial decisions at all. I have no idea whether Otto Brusiin would agree with my conclusions this evening, but I am confident that he would approve of my choice of subject and my attempt to derive more universal conclusions from it. Let me end with his own words:

> "A fruitful legal theory should take its departure from everyday legal phenomena. The factual background of the thinking of every scholar in this domain is formed by his personal experiences within the law machinery of his country."[20]

... and then...

> "Legal theory is international in principle: the same fundamental problems are investigated in different countries."[21]

---

20 *Brusiin* (note 18), p. 466.
21 Ibid., p. 469.

RECHTSTHEORIE 28 (1997), S. 157 - 165
Duncker & Humblot, 12165 Berlin

JURIDICAL THINKING, JURIDICAL DECISION-MAKING*

By Hermann Klenner, Berlin

Without wanting to annoy you with my personal sentiments, I cannot help starting with an homage to a man of learning and his native country. He was the very first scholar from a foreign country who, some 35 years ago, broke through my own intellectual isolation, a result of fate and fault – my socialist fate and my personal fault – by forwarding to me on presentation a copy of one of his treatises. I am, of course, speaking of Otto Brusiin. The title of the treatise read *Über das juristische Denken,* and it has been the inspiration of my lecture today.[1] I don't know why Brusiin felt obliged to give me this monograph, and later others as well, even more so because each time he would inscribe on the cover a dedication that I did not deserve. I was at that time about 26 years old, Brusiin being 20 years older than me. I must confess that, at that time and even later, I was following a path led by Hegel whereas Brusiin was never a Hegelian thinker. I was then, and later as well, above all interested in changing and revolutionising society and law whereas he wanted to understand and comprehend society and law. So it is understandable that, in those days, Brusiin impressed me more with the international character of his legal and theoretical sources, with the global nature of his considerations, than with his anthropological approach, more with his methods than with his results. And if I compared his monographs[2] with many of the notable contemporary treatises in the field of legal theory – including my own –, I would inevitably come to the conclusion that most of us were both poor and presumptuous, poor because we did not look into the legislation and the judicature of other countries before elaborating our own ideas, and foolhardy because we were confident in the generality – or even universality – of our findings and conclusions without having looked close enough across the borders of our own legal polities. Brusiin's rejection of provincialism together with his vast historical knowledge enabled him to become what

---

* Dedicated to the heirs of Otto Brusiin, to my colleagues and friends in Finland.

1 *O. Brusiin,* Über das juristische Denken, Helsingfors 1951.

2 *Brusiin,* Über die Objektivität der Rechtsprechung, Helsinki 1949; *Brusiin,* Zum Ehescheidungsproblem, Hyvinkää 1959; *Brusiin,* Zum Problem des immateriellen Schadens, Turku 1966.

he was: one of the finest and most perceptive legal scholars of this century. And to end these personal remarks, it was Brusiin who was, in the final analysis, responsible for the fact that, for the first time in my life, I read an academic book in a foreign language from the first line to the last in one stroke. It was a monograph in English but written by a Finnish scholar: Georg Henrik von Wright's *Norm and Action.*[3]

As Aulis Aarnio has pointed out in his essay on the development of legal theory and the philosophy of law in Finland, Brusiin was a persistent searcher, seer and educator in Finnish legal culture.[4] I am not the right person to confirm this assertion, to say nothing of contesting it. But what I am able to affirm is that Brusiin marks the beginning of the international reputation of Finnish jurisprudence!

Brusiin commenced his career as an outstanding scholar with his dissertation on the problem of gap-filling by judges published in 1938.[5] Although I did find a copy in the State Library in Berlin, I was unfortunately unable to read it because of my ignorance of the language in which it was written, a language with such a pleasant tone. But gap-filling by judges does belong to my topic, i.e., juridical thinking and juridical decision-making.

My favourite poet (at least of this century) Bertolt Brecht, a friend of the admirable Finn Hella Wuolijoki who helped Brecht as well as Brusiin in times when they needed support for political reasons – her memoirs have recently been published in German[6] –, once wrote: *"Das Denken gehört zu den größten Vergnügungen der menschlichen Rasse."* Thinking belongs to the greatest pleasures of the human race. But he also wrote in a dialogue written during his emigration in Finland but published only after his death in Berlin: *"Scharfes Denken ist schmerzhaft."* Acute thinking is painful.[7]

Where should I index juridical thinking, under the pleasures or the pains? Before answering this seriously meant question, I must at least indicate what I mean by *juridical* thinking. To be a lawyer is a respectable profession, and it has even been said that, of all the professions, the lawyer has the biggest possibility to participate in the exercise of political power. I could, accordingly, confine myself to stipulating that juridical thinking is the intellectual work done by jurists, i.e., making legal rules of behaviour, delivering and pronouncing judgements, decisions or

---

3 *G. H. von Wright,* Norm and Action, London 1963.

4 *A. Aarnio,* Philosophical Perspectives in Jurisprudence, Helsinki 1983, p. 17.

5 *Brusiin,* Tuomarin harkinta normin puuttuessa, Vammala 1938.

6 *H. Wuolijoki,* Und ich war nicht Gefangene, Rostock 1987, p. 228.

7 *B. Brecht,* Leben des Galilei, in: Werke, Band 5, Berlin/Frankfurt 1988, p. 211; *Brecht,* Flüchtlingsgespräche, Berlin 1962, p. 101.

sentences, the professional reasoning of lawyers be they prosecutors, solicitors, barristers or judges or even professors of law. Brusiin specifically differentiated between the juridical thinking of judges (aiming to settle a case) and of attorneys-at-law or of counsels. Some take the judicial decision – and the intellectual process formulating it – as *the* paradigm of legal decision, and, of course, they are entitled to do so.

But what are the common features of the different kinds of juridical thinking? What distinguishes the lawyer's thinking from the physician's, the physicist's or the economist's thinking? And are there real differences, for thinking is the *logical* use of the mind in order to form opinions and to come to conclusions? And is logic not the science of absolute truths? Why should there exist a special branch of logic for jurists? And, on the other hand, if Ulpianus was right in saying that *"iurisprudentia est divinarum atque humanarum rerum notitia, iusti atque iniusti scientia"*,[8] then there is nothing between heaven and earth that could not be a possible subject or object of legal reflections and decisions.

In my mind – with no pretensions of comprehensiveness and exactitude –, juridical thinking is, at the very least, characterised by five aspects. Juridical thinking is oriented:

a) towards rationality,

b) towards conflict,

c) towards interests,

d) towards law, and, finally,

e) towards decision-making.

It is the combination of these five properties – or rather "peculiarities" – that distinguishes thinking as juridical.

Juridical thinking is, *firstly,* oriented towards rationality. I fully agree with MacCormick's thesis that rationality in law and in legal processes is the first virtue.[9] A problem, however, remains unsolved: What is rationality? Is the capacity of orderly, procedural thinking sufficient? Are we satisfied with a mere functional rationalism, or should we, perhaps, aspire to a substantial rationality? Rationality *is,* at any rate, a precondition for a scientific approach and – this should not be underestimated – for communication between partners, contractors and participants within the legal process of legislation as well as of the administration of justice. There is, after all, a certain connection between the rule of law and the rule of reason. Max Weber was right in emphasising this point with which Brusiin *expressis verbis* agreed (op. cit., p. 113).

---

[8] Dig. 1, 1, 10, 2.

[9] *N. MacCormick,* Legal Right and Social Democracy, Oxford 1984, pp. 64, 96.

There is no autonomy of rationality because arguing rationally always means working out presupposed premises or, at its best, comparing thoughts on reality with reality itself. But without rationality it is impossible to discover these premises and facts of life and to argue in favour of them or against them.

Rationality is a result of knowledge and, at the same time, a means to broaden the scope of knowledge. On the other hand, knowing little means believing much. If belief divides mankind, knowledge unites it or, at least, inclines to do so. It seems to me that this understanding is the very reason why Brusiin resolutely supported a "methodological atheism", as he put it (cf. note 1, p. 161).

I am, of course, well aware of the unfortunate fact that there are judges – let alone counsels – who first *make* the decision and only later invent the reasons for it. I cannot deny that emotions and feelings sometimes represent experiences. But with emotions one can justify absolutely everything. I am certainly not against feelings for feelings are a part of man. But reasonable remedies are needed against uncontrollable affections, as Spinoza taught us in his *Ethica* (V, 2; 4), at least if you have to take responsibility for other people.

Juridical thinking is, *secondly*, oriented towards conflict. If there are no conflicts in society, law is unnecessary. Sometimes legislators have been obsessed with the idea that only they can provide or create relations between men that are free of quarrels, disputes, actions, suits and conflicts. Experience has shown that such an idea has always turned out to be an illusion. Laws, statutes and judgments cannot produce a harmonious society. Law can only relatively harmonise the way in which the inevitable contradictions are to be solved effectively and with humane methods and, as a means, contribute to the minimising and neutralising of arisen conflicts.

Law is simply overburdened by the task that it has been given, i.e., to bring about a conflict-free society. As a rule, contradictions are not the result of bad or poor law, but laws are the product of unavoidable contradictions. There is a painful truth in Marx's paradoxical remark that, just as the poet produces poems, the criminal produces laws, courts and even the authors of textbooks on the penal code (MEGA II/3, p. 280). Juridical thinking is, therefore, inseparably linked to social conflicts, and only such legislators and judges have learned their lesson well whose imagination is enriched with the numerous, diverse and, yet, feasible conflicts that their statutes and judgments will produce. It is the fate of scholars to create new problems by solving old ones. It is the fate of lawyers to create new conflicts by overcoming old ones.

In the long run, there is *both* stagnation *and* progress in law as well as in science. But one cannot define progress in terms of a science of law without having incorporated man and mankind into that concept and perspective. The living conditions of man, his/her productivity and creativeness, these are the things which, in the last analysis, count.

Law serves mankind empirically during its evolutionary and revolutionary periods as a yardstick of human behaviour. But if one inquires into the yardstick for the yardstick called "law", into what legitimises and illegitimises law, one should, first and foremost, look into the development of the material and intellectual living conditions of the common man, into the everyday life of people and their possibility to display their capacities. Just as the physician, the lawyer should never forget that it is the people that must pay for his activities, inactivities and misconducts.

Juridical thinking is, *thirdly,* oriented towards interests. Different opinions, views, values, needs, demands and requirements in society reflect on diverse interests. Private interests are socially determined, as well, because they can only be satisfied within the conditions set and by the means given by the established society. The legislator and the judge have no possibility to adopt a point or a position outside the interests of this world. Sometimes legal theorists and philosophers of law are inclined to forget that, in addition to thoughts, experiences continuously influence our thinking. This is due to the omnipresence of social and individual interests. Before we start thinking, we must live, and we live by the truth of our five senses.

We should, then, not be too puzzled by the clearly observable fact that the rationality involved in the process of making and executing law is at least slightly distorted by established interests. In the end, law itself is a measure *and* an expression of interests, of the dominating interests in a given society. As to the social relations in which law partakes, there is no conceivable – let alone available – dialogue, polylogue or discourse that would be completely free of man's domination over another, not even in an academic seminar, to say nothing of a trial against a traitor or a terrorist. And the judge would not be regarded as human if his/her heart did not beat on the left or the other side – politically speaking – of his/her chest.

A lawyer's virtue is to think and act unbiased, unprejudiced and impartially. It is an aim that should be consistently desired, striving for it is worthy. But what about the impartiality of a judge if the legislator is partial? Can, for instance, the legislator think and act impartially in relation to the question of abortion, the death penalty, or property, or in relation to the simple question of whether one prefers unemployment to higher inflation? What is the smallest common denominator between the weak and the strong, the poor and the rich, the exploited and the exploiter, the tortured and the torturer, the oppressed and his/her oppressor? Are both sides only interested in their own life? In any established society, there are fundamentalists with whom no compromise is possible. The judge's freedom from prejudice does not guarantee that he/she will not prejudice someone. Precedents are as charged with prejudice as statutes.

My intention here is not to offer solutions but rather to diminish illusions. In hard cases, juridical thinking is much like squaring the circle. It has been said that the well-known differentiation between hard and simple cases is absurd, that there are only cheap and expensive cases because a gifted and, accordingly, well-paid legal counsel is able to transform any case into a hard case. True, I may be exaggerating, but sometimes it is preferable to overdo than to understate. A continuous consensus presupposes interests that can be generalised. Today the survival of mankind requires that this undeniable truth is acknowledged.

Juridical thinking is, *fourthly,* oriented towards law. Contrary to all appearances, this is not a truism. The lawyer's thinking takes place within the boundaries of an established law or aims to replace, to substitute old law with new law. It is a thinking about chains in chains: *in vinculis esse.*[10] Although the chains are wrapped in concordant words and legitimised with godlike values, they are delivered and supervised by an earthly power. Is the lawyer, then, only the legislator's footman? Is he/she by definition conservative? Is he/she a rational technologist simply placing his/her skills at the disposal of others, especially of those who hold the reins of political, economical and ideological power? Is this the core of their activities, is their actual job executing domination in a plausible way? Does he/she, as the raw material of politicians, belong to those who understand nothing but decide everything?

I will not deny that there have been, at all times and in all countries, lawyers who have behaved exactly so, but I cannot help considering them unscrupulous accomplices. In the words of Christopher Marlowe: "Their study fits a mercenary drudge/Who aims at nothing but external trash/Too servile and illiberal for me." (Doctor Faustus I, 1.)

Coming from a country where – in theory – there is no judge-made law, I would, nevertheless, insist upon a relationship between the judge and the law. Judges do not simply execute statutes. Despite Montesquieu's famous dictum that, in a sense, judicial power does not exist *(en quelque*

10 Dig. 4, 6, 9.

façon nulle), one should keep in mind that general rules do not decide particular cases and judges do not supply empty bottles with contents. Because the legislator is required, at least in modern times, to accommodate to the democratic spirit of the age, the text of the constitutions as well as of other fundamental statutes have become sufficiently inexact – mercifully inexact, I might add. Therefore it seems both unwise and ill-advised to deny the vast scope of creative activity within the established legality. There is a domain of an alternative jurisprudence and law. There is room left for an evolution of law "from below". I do not urge an *agere in fraudem legis* by judges (with important exceptions, of course, such as fascist statutes). One should expect neither good nor virtue from a judiciary that ventures to mould, shape and twist the laws into any form it pleases. But I have every reason to assume that Brusiin would not have had any objections against an evolution of the legal polity by lawyers "from below". It is not by chance that approximately half of the endorsers of the Declaration of Independence of the USA were lawyers, and the juridical work done "from below" by the great Karl Liebknecht, Mahatma Gandhi and Denis Nowell Pritt, each an attorney-at-law for the oppressed, should never be forgotten, either.

Taking rights seriously means primarily taking democracy and emancipation seriously. But please note: democracy for the people by the people, and the emancipation of man by man. If *in dubio pro libertate,*[11] then why not *in dubio pro aequalitate,* too? If *in dubio pro reo iudicandum est,*[12] why not *in dubio* favour the weak, the poor, the exploited, the colonised? In theory, physicians swear an oath to Hippocrates. Lawyers should – in practice – take an oath to Papinianus who made "in doubt favour liberty" a legal principle and was murdered by Caracalla because he resisted tyranny. It is a lawyer's responsibility to use his/her discretion and his/her brains. But in whose interests? We are not at liberty to forget that to become a lawyer also means taking a risk.

Juridical thinking is, *lastly,* oriented towards decision-making. This aspect leads us into further contradictions. Within the process of legislation and judicature, reasoning serves as a precondition of decision-making. It is not an end in itself, but neither is it merely a preliminary stage that prepares new thoughts. On the contrary, reasoning has to be brought to an end, for what finally matters is the decision, the resolution, the judgment, the verdict, the sentence, the acquittal, the decree, the act, the statute. Descriptions have to be transformed into prescriptions. And there is seldom enough time available for making law in gen-

11 Dig. 50, 70, 20.

12 Dig. 42, 1, 38 pr.

eral and prescribing an order in particular. "But what if you don't know?", asked Sophocles' Kreon, and Oedipus answered: "I must govern..." Usually a judge cannot wait until a consensus between the litigants has been reached. He/she represents the consensus of the community, a fictitious consensus. To reflect in science – at least in the field of pure research – means reaching out for the infinite, but legal reasoning must be completed in a rather short time. It begins with an order and terminates with one, as well. And this is the crux. As to the *theory* of law, there is no *res judicata,* whereas in the *practice* of law, *res judicata* is needed. One never knows enough in deciding hard cases. But hard cases require a decision as urgently as simple ones, and that is why juridical thinking is sometimes so painful. Sometimes it has to stop at the very beginning. That is why legalising behaviour is easier than legitimising a legislative or a judicial decision. What distinguishes an inspired lawyer is that he/she never regards the juridical decision merely as the *result* of juridical thinking but also as a new beginning for it. This means turning the outcome of reasoning into its commencement.

I fully realise that my five "peculiarities" of juridical thinking – I could add others – do not provide a closed picture of law as it is. But it is not likely that a theory in the field of the social sciences that contains no contradictions and leaves no problems unsolved would reflect social reality correctly. Sooner or later the accuracy of any theory offering a closed system of methods and results is lost. There is an inevitable moment in which one must comprehend the truth of the romanticist paradox that a system is as deadly as the lack thereof.

What I wanted to demonstrate with my rather fragmentary remarks is the appropriateness of Brusiin's notion that *"das juristische Denken ist von der sozialen Gesamtsituation abhängig"* (p. 133). Because he never overlooked the overall social context in which law is embedded, he gave so much value and importance – despite Jhering and Kelsen – to causality in life and in law. He *expressis verbis* attacked all those who considered jurists incorporating the question of causality into their deliberations as pure – and therefore poor – sociologists of law.

Hence, it follows that juridical thinking must transgress law in order to understand it. The transformation of non-law into law, as well as the transformation of law into social life, cannot be excluded from the field of jurisprudence. Legal dogmatics, philosophy of law, theory of law, sociology of law, psychology of law, axiology of law, anthropology of law, ethnology of law, ethology of law, and history of law (including the history of juridical ideas), they all need one another. Each is incomplete in itself and offers only an incomplete picture of law. It is, therefore, indispensable for any discipline of jurisprudence to preserve law as a real object of analysis in a genetic, structural and functional relationship. Any reductionism, i.e., the reduction of the problematics with one of the three mentioned aspects, leads to a distortion of reality. Jurisprudence, like all the other branches of science, is only justified by its proximity to reality.

Juridical thinking is a challenge to us all. It is, to take up Brecht's characterisation once again, full of both pleasures and pains. In the *pains,* I include, first and foremost, our inefficiency, incapacity and incapability to eliminate the inhumane elements of human society during our own lifetime. The contradictions in our conceptions, interpretations and options belong to the *pleasures*. It has, therefore, been not only an honour but a great pleasure to exchange, on different occasions, dissimilar and sometimes even contradictory views with that marvellous scholar to whom I will leave the final words. Otto Brusiin said that juridical thinking

> *"hat heroische Anstrengungen gemacht. Die schärfsten Gehirne waren am Werk. Alles vergebens. Es tobt ein ewiger Kampf zwischen den verschiedenen Theorien, und dieser Kampf hat etwas Besonderes: eine Entscheidung scheint heute ebensofern zu liegen wie am ersten Tag."*[13]

---

[13] Cf. note 1, p. 156.

RECHTSTHEORIE 28 (1997), S. 167 - 201
Duncker & Humblot, 12165 Berlin

THEORY AND RESEARCH PROGRAMME OF LEGAL EXPERIENCE

Otto Brusiin's General Theory of Law

By Werner Krawietz, Münster

It is difficult to say with any confidence what the general public is and what role it plays in politics and culture, in the economy and in society, and it is particularly difficult in the case of a democratic society organized along state lines. If one follows Habermas when he suggests that the concept and word "general public" are to be understood collectively and that various general publics are to be distinguished,[1] then it is perhaps the scientific or research-oriented public that deserves, today, the greatest attention in contemporary society. And I am prepared to say this in spite of my doubts about how far the possibilities of immediately realizing the effects of science extend. It is not often that we have occasion to doubt the power of innovation in science, since impulses both for self-renewal and for the reform of law and society stem from science.[2] If science and research are really to be counted among the important and significant forms of production of our society, it is also the scientific and research-oriented public that points out to us which tendencies determine contemporary and future development.

A new publication of various writings by Otto Brusiin, writings that have profoundly shaped discussion in contemporary legal theory for a some time, deserves special attention. The work in question is his book *Man and His Law,* in German, *Der Mensch und sein Recht,* published a short time ago.[3] With this publication both the editor and publisher honour, posthumously, this author, who in fact wrote his most significant works in German.

---

1 *Jürgen Habermas,* Strukturwandel der Öffentlichkeit (Frankfurt a.M. 1990), pp. 21ff., 33ff., 38f.

2 *Werner Krawietz,* "Zur Struktur von Entwicklung und Fortschritt in der Rechtstheorie", in: Ilmar Tammelo/Aulis Aarnio (eds.), Zum Fortschritt von Theorie und Technik in Recht und Ethik (Berlin 1981), pp. 333 - 347, 337f., 342f.

3 *Otto Brusiin,* Der Mensch und sein Recht. Ausgewählte rechtstheoretische Schriften, ed. with an intro. by Urpo Kangas (Berlin 1990).

I. General Legal Theory as Theory of Legal Communities

1. Brusiin's investigations in the field of legal theory appear today in a volume whose contents are summarized in the title "Man and Law". It appears at a time during which a number of state legal systems in central Europe – I think above all of Hungary, Czechoslovakia and what was the German Democratic Republic – have managed to shake themselves free of the yoke of a socialistic, one-party system. Today they face the task of bringing the prevailing legal system of the past into line with the changed conditions brought about by the peaceful revolution of 1989. This is not something that can be accomplished simply by a show of strength on the part of the state. Rather, the required transformation will be brought about only by means of profound self-renewal and a reorganization of *all* the social forces at hand. Perhaps the conditions for a far-reaching reception of Brusiin's legal theory are therefore more favourable today than they were in the situation in which Finland and Germany found themselves at the end of the Second World War.

The same is true for a number of other legal systems organized along state lines. That is to say, to the degree to which theoretical inquiries into the structure of the law have remained, right up to the present day, a prisoner of traditional, merely conventional notions of a theoretically inadequate form of self-reflection, it would appear that here, too, a renewal of legal thinking is necessary.

2. In the works published here, Brusiin's breakthrough to a theory of law emerges clearly. The insights that he developed have yielded nothing of their originality and pertinence over the years, as even a cursory examination will show. On the contrary, the international discussion of the last two decades, greatly promoted through Brusiin's research and discoveries, has in my view shown that a number of problems to which he had turned his attention remain, today, without satisfactory answers. This makes it possible – and also necessary – to enter once again into a dialogue with Brusiin's legal theory.

a) Otto Brusiin's *Man and His Law* contains the programmatic essay "On Legal Theory", which first appeared in 1947, but which is only now appearing in German. Here Brusiin sketches the cognitive and scientific programme of the "general legal theory" that he defended ever since. According to the theory, the law, "if seen from the standpoint not of its content but of its structure, is alike in all communities". There are, too, comparable communities existing apart from the state and independently of the state. Since the law as the guiding principle of human behaviour structures *all* social relations and societal formations, all such communities according to their form are legal communities. It is to them that these remarks are addressed. The volume now appearing also includes Brusiin's two monographic inquiries "On the Objectivity of Adjudication" and "On Legal Thinking", first appearing in German in 1949 and 1951 respectively. Pretty clearly, they are Brusiin's most significant works in the field. I might add, in passing, that the volume also offers a glimpse of Brusiin's entire *œuvre,* this in the form of a bibliography of his writings. Here we find not only a complete enumeration of his writings in legal theory but also a list of the various reviews of his works, making it possible to follow the national and international reception to Brusiin at the time his writings appeared. I will consider the impact of Brusiin's work in other contexts in the course of my remarks; it goes without saying that I will be able to document its impact only in part.

b) The book also contains an "Introduction to the Legal Thought of Otto Brusiin" written by Professor Urpo Kangas. This thoughtful and probing inquiry – practically a book within a book – counts in its balanced and carefully differentiated account as the best of everything I have read to date on the character, life, and work of Otto Brusiin. I am confident that this "Introduction" will have a welcome and fruitful impact on future discussion of Brusiin's legal theory.

3. To be sure, as researchers and scholars it does not lie within our own power to determine whether our work will command any attention at all. Nor do we have a voice in how, and when, such a reception might take place. Also – and this has special import in the case of the law and legal thinking – there are, typically, only a handful of publications that enjoy any sort of reception from a broader public, namely, beyond national boundaries, with an impact, then, that is transnational in nature. Without any doubt, Otto Brusiin belongs to that small group of legal thinkers who have succeeded in renewing, influencing and in leaving their imprint on modern legal thought – not legal thought as it is seen simply from the legal culture of this or that state but, indeed, legal thought as seen internationally. One does not have to be a prophet to see that as modern legal theory makes further progress, Brusiin's theory, too – above all as considered internationally – will have a great impact.

II. Basic Concepts, Levels, and Stages of Theorizing in Legal Thinking

1. At the forefront of Otto Brusiin's reflections, the question is posed: How is the law found in individual cases? This is, indeed, the question posed by jurists the world over. One wants to know what the law comes to in *this* or in *that* concrete case – what *ought,* legally speaking, to be held in this individual case. It is a central part of the Continental-European persuasion that in the course of answering this question, Otto

Brusiin ought to be led by an orientation toward the existing legal system – in particular, by an orientation to legislation, to the statute. The Continental-European predilection for the general and abstract rule, characteristically preceding the decision in the case at hand – a general rule, expressed above all in statutes and codes, but also in other forms of legal norm – turns the ongoing reproduction and objectification of the law into the central theme and problematic of legal thought. To be sure, this first becomes clear after one has transferred the whole of legal practice, that is to say, *all* forms of the application of legal norms *qua* legal rules that are in fact employed, into the field of modern basic research – in a word, into legal theory.

a) Adjudication constantly monitors the daily fare of legal life, namely, the ongoing processes of identifying and complying with legal rules, and it feeds the decisional component back into the legal system as factual and normative information. In so doing, adjudication moves to stage center as the primary theme, the central theme, of legal theory. And – as with the clarity the natural scientist enjoys in looking into a burning glass – in adjudication *all* the social forces involved in the creation of law and that are, therefore, normatively efficacious are focused. However, Brusiin's cognitive interests are not restricted to the central – and in the modern *Rechtsstaat,* most important – field of law alongside legislation, namely adjudication, which in the continuing judicial creation of law – here understood as the permanent "objectifying" of the law – attains in the form of judicial decisions its "objectification".

b) And the *grand design* of Brusiin's theory of law is constituted by the fact that at all the various levels of legal development and the development of jurisprudential thought – beyond all "experts" in legal dogmatics, as he put it – he made a place for the entry of science into the law, his theory of the law. It is precisely here that the second great theme of his life's work and achievement is found. Perhaps the present summary of his most important writings in legal theory, which brings the points of his theory together in a mosaic – points initially developed in separation from each other – will show more clearly than before what is at issue in Brusiin's theory.

2. From the very beginning, Brusiin had written the most important and most essential parts of his works in legal theory in German; at the center of this work one finds a theory of the legal community. His style is captivating in its conceptual pregency and in the clarity that he brings to the systematic development of his ideas. Astonishingly, his inquiries in legal theory, from which anglo-american legal theory, too, might profit, have not been translated into English, not even selections. To be sure, a translation would pose difficulties of a linguistic nature; these stem,

however, from the peculiarities of and difficulties in the two languages and are not to be attributed to the author. A reader not at home in German will encounter difficulties too. When Otto Brusiin speaks of a "human being" *("Mensch")* and of his law *("sein Recht"),* he is thinking not foremost and not alone of the concrete, individual human being, but of the "human being" as a *social* species. When he speaks of "his law", he does not mean the subjective right of a certain person in the sense of an individual right *("subjektives Recht"),* but the objective law *("objektives Recht"),* that is to say, the legal system, addressed to a plurality of individuals. The expressions "the law" and "legal system" are used by Brusiin – unless something else is specified – as meaning the same thing. As he writes, "'the law' and 'legal system' are therefore synonymous in our linguistic usage". And when he speaks with reference to the human being, speaking of "his" law, he means thereby the social species of human being – that is to say, all law is the product of human beings alone and is thus made exclusively by human beings and for human beings, even where it is not intentionally and deliberately created.

a) Seen methodologically, Brusiin proceeds here inductively in that he orients himself to the daily experience and action of the individual and proceeds from the particular to the general. His legal theory focuses, from the point of view of a participant observer, on observing, describing and interpreting the normatively influenced and directed regularities of human behaviour in the everyday legal life of the citizen or, alternatively, of the bureaucratically engaged state legal staffs, and in this way arrives, in the form of inductive abstractions and careful generalizations, at social "law-like regularities".[4] In this way he is also in a position to abstract and to generalize the human being into a social species, without thereby leaving or going beyond the field of possible experience. His point of departure from both the everyday life of the law and the individual, the experience and action of the individual to which experience and observation are accessible, gives rise to be sure to another problem. We run up against the difficulty that all these activities of people and officials are human activities and are therefore carried on according to certain norms and rules, as a participant observer can see without any difficulty. There is, however, as Brusiin never tires of emphasizing, a great lack of recognition that the law – understood as a social institution or a socio-legal system – involves far more than simply the normative

[4] These law-like regularities are, it is well to note, *only* to be understood as recurring structural patterns, as they represent themselves for a particular observer or for the legal theorist who absorbs this experience and observation and reflects critically on it. See *Brusiin,* Der Mensch und sein Recht (note 3), 56ff., 62f., 65. Therefore they have nothing whatever to do with any sort of "natural" or "non-human" or, indeed, "universal" *laws* that would have to be seen as such even in the absence of any human intervention.

codifying and conditioning of human forms of action and regularities of behaviour in procedures that serve the regulated settlement as well as the resolution of and decisions on legal conflicts. It is precisely here that Brusiin's theory of legal communities comes into play.

b) Brusiin therefore has nothing in common with the natural law philosophers and philosophers of reason from the seventeenth and eighteenth centuries or with their successors. These thinkers accepted "nature" or pure "reason" as guides; with the help of these guides, they believed they could cognize the "natural laws", so to speak, of the legal life world of human beings, laws arising without human intervention that were to serve a putatively natural, or at any rate reasonable process of rendering perfect the social forms of life.

aa) As his now published theory of law makes clear, Brusiin is also no representative of contemporary, albeit long outmoded contractualism, be it the "natural law" variety or that of "reason", which claims to be able to cognize the foundations of the law in a contract (social contract, state contract, contract of subjugation) between human (rational) beings. And he has nothing in common with the contemporary representatives and heirs of a contract theory that offers us new variations on the theme of a contractual model. Indeed, the contract theory, seen from the standpoint of the social sciences, is an altogether unsatisfactory conceptual model, one without explanatory value. Nor, therefore, does Brusiin share the credo of the proponents of contractualism who believe, even today, that the foundations of all law are supposed to be cognized – if not in an actual contract, that is, a willfully concluded contract, then in any case in a merely hypothetical and thus fictitious contract, presupposed as a command of reason, a contract whose presumed validity, or the validity reasonably to be presumed, binds by its very nature every rational being who is capable of such cognition with every other rational being.

bb) Brusiin, for his part, is of the view that in the legal community there was, at the beginning of all thought and action, no contract between human beings. There is also no directive of reason (whose reason? which reason?) that imposes such a contract binding on all human beings, citizens, or subjects of state power, as contemporary contractualism would have us believe.[5] And, where an actual contract does not exist, no hypothetical contract is capable of serving as the presupposition of a contractually based legal community either. Rather, non-con-

---

5 See for a critique of the older, contractually grounded communal thinking in political theory *Peter Koller,* Neue Theorien des Sozialkontrakts (Berlin 1987), 15 ff. et passim; *Werner Krawietz,* "Kontraktualismus oder Konsozialismus?", RECHTSTHEORIE Beiheft 7 (1988), 391 - 423, at 403 f.

tractual bases, namely, for Brusiin, the social causes, reasons, and other factors lying at the societal basis of the law, must be investigated.

c) Obviously Brusiin, too, takes as his point of departure the fact that the law – seen from the standpoint of linguistics and the philosophy of language – is typically set down in normative sentences. They give expression to the legal norm, with whose meaning and normative sense legal practice as well as practical legal science are engaged. Brusiin, however, takes up a distinction here – a truly remarkable distinction from the standpoint of legal theory. "In connection with theoretical research on law, a distinction should be made between the legal norm and the linguistic form in which the legal norm appears." Brusiin, however, does not reduce the legal norm and the legal point of view to an analysis of uses of legal language or to the purely normative meaning or the juridico-linguistic sense of these sentences. He is, therefore, not to be numbered among those authors who see in the law only conceptual content, which by its very nature would not be accessible to human experience and observation. For him, the law in the first instance is a social "structure" or the normative structure of the social forms of life. As such, it is identifiable "in a variety of historically given communities". All law according to its structure is always an integrative component of the social order, but it is also only *one* such component, that is to say, there are also other social components that – together with the law – ensure the identity, the existence, and the further development of the society. And this social order is at the same time a historical order, that is, an order of social life created by human beings *qua* social species, and this order – although made by human beings for human beings – does not underlie, not at any rate in its totality, the intentional and purposive disposition of the individual or of different social systems. All legal communities are social systems of interaction and organization between human beings, to whose normative structure the law, too, belongs; and all legal communities, thus understood, are based on the kind of historico-social order described here. Seen from the standpoint of the philosophy of science, the object of basic research in law is, therefore, the "law" itself, understood as the "class formed out of all conceivable positive legal systems". It is a matter, then, *not* of a simple *in mente* existing and merely *ideal* normative law but always of law that socio-structurally exists in fact – of law that is actually efficacious today and is, *pro futuro,* actually possible.

aa) Abstracting from their respective legal content, Brusiin's theory of law seeks to comprehend and to describe the legal structure as a product of social organization, whose elements – recurring again and again in the various legal systems – are factually "ascertainable". In this connection, the point of departure and foundation of Brusiin's legal theory is the concrete "legal experience" of the individual human being.

bb) Brusiin's concern is with the construction of a structural theory of law, which deals not only with the linguistic structure of the legal system but also with its societal *deep structure,* which underlies all social systems. For Brusiin the law is therefore *one* normative structure of society, that is, the object of his legal theory is not the legal sentence or the legal norm in its juridico-linguistic meaning, its purely normative sense alone, namely, that which is at issue in levels 1 - 3 of the scheme on legal thinking described and explained by Brusiin (and restated below).[6] Rather, he is concerned with the legal norm in the form in which it is complied with, namely through human action; this is the legal norm *qua* legal rule, which for its part has always been of social coinage. In any case, it is true of norm compliance and especially of compliance with law that one who complies with a legal norm, namely, by applying it to the situation calling for a decision, has a possibility of participating in, or following up on, a form of reflection carried out, or to be carried out, in legal thought. Thus, in Brusiin's theory of law the connection of norm and action finds its way to stage center.

3. For Brusiin, the social life of the human being is not only a field of individual practical action. It is, above all – as I have already pointed out – a broad, social field, that is, a field of rule-governed and rule-guided action. However, while we explain much of people's behaviour in terms of rule-following or rule-breaking or rule-making, we cannot explain all of it in this way. The regularities of social behaviour – clearly recognizable to the participating observer – that result from rule-following do not, as such, exemplify some sort of natural or social "laws". Neither rules nor regularities finding expression in social action influenced by norms are laws in the sense familiar from the natural sciences. All social "law-like regularities" of this nature that determine and govern the social order – Brusiin likes to speak, here, of "constants" or "invariants" in order to emphasize their socio-structural autonomy – are man-made. Here, too, man is understood as a social species, even if we are not always in a position precisely to designate, to describe, and to explain its historical and social origin. Thus, one has no occasion to assume that this legal system and its social "law-like regularities" are an expression of extra-human, invariable or universal laws of nature. If, however, this is the case, then – and here lies Brusiin's pathbreaking insight – one must take leave of legal science and its "general" legal theory, heretofore too narrowly limited to the law, and turn with an eye

---

6 See at IV 2 a) - d), below.

to the relation of norms *and* action to social research. To be sure, the question then arises: What can a theory of law *and* society contribute to this cluster of issues? And is this legal theory in a position to describe and explain the structure and functions of law more adequately? It is precisely here that the achievement of Brusiin's theory is found.

a) This is not the place to explore the various sources from which Brusiin arrived at his important insights in legal theory. In the critical exchange with the normativism of traditional legal positivism, especially in the exchange with Kelsen, Brusiin's efforts to arrive at his own position were assisted by conversations with his friends Osvi Lahtinen and Jan-Magnus Jansson, as Brusiin himself reports. However – as he satisfied himself by examining North American and Scandinavian legal realism – a merely "sociologically inspired positivistic science" of that stripe was not in a position to carry out a "social task", which is the idea that Brusiin had brought to the fore. In order to refine and make more precise his new position in legal theory, it was – as best one can judge the matter – Belgian, French, and Italian theorists who made the key contributions, such as Jean Haesart and Husson, Carnelutti, Cicala and Bagolini, along with Spanish and Argentine authors such as Legaz y Lacambra and Carlos Cossio. One should not, however, overestimate their influence on Brusiin's own original position.

b) In my view, Brusiin's legal theory draws on insights that are represented, above all, in sociological jurisprudence and – in the theory and sociology of law since Ihering – by Max Weber. It is no coincidence that Max Weber is the most frequently cited author, in Brusiin's work, after Kelsen and Stammler. One cannot help but be struck, too, by the fact – as a glance at the index of the new edition makes clear – that the most frequently cited authors are those who represent a sociological view of the law or have, at any rate, affinities to such a view. I think in this connection of Eugen Ehrlich, Franz Jerusalem, Theodor Geiger, Gurvitsch, Timasheff and of course Barna Horvath, and Leon Petraczycki, whom Brusiin characterizes with special honour and respect as a "genius among legal theorists". Precisely the latter is, however, a theorist who in his theory of law gives free reign to reflections from sociology.

III. Norms and Action from the Perspective of a Theory of Legal Experience

The point of departure of Brusiin's legal theory is "legal experience". By this he means, in the case of the legal theorist, the "personal" legal experience that the researcher, too, possesses "from his own positive law system". The legal system in which he himself lives is for him, however, only the "raw material". Even if this may present, "at first glance, a manifold equally great in magnitude", this is no barrier for the theory of law and society. For the legal theorist, the main emphasis always lies with the "structural questions". Among the fundamental concepts with whose help Brusiin confirms the socio-structural "law-like regularities" that are characteristic of every legal system, there are above all three key concepts: (i) the concept of practical *uses of law,* (ii) the concept of the *objectification* of law, and (iii) the concept of *introspection* that underlies all possible legal experience.

1. Oriented to the interplay of norms and action, an interplay that is to be observed in everyday life, Brusiin takes as his point of departure the "empirical fact" that – at least in the modern cultural state but also in earlier stages of the social development of the law – there are always practical "uses of law" that one can describe, interpret, and explain. It is always a matter, here, of action oriented to norms – oriented, that is, to "practical activity". This makes it both possible and necessary to consider the "legal community" – from the standpoint of a theoretical analysis – "under the aspect of repeatedly recurring types of these practical uses".

a) As examples of "types of practical uses of law", Brusiin has in mind – alongside the "uses of law" supplied through lay persons, that is, citizens – the "uses of law", above all, that are manifested in one's professional capacity, that is, "every activity of the practical jurist that has something to do with law". Here Brusiin is thinking not only of the activity of advocacy especially on behalf of lay persons, but above all of the legislative, administrative, and judicial activities carried out by jurists in their professional capacity. Judicial activity in particular takes on, for him, "a key position in the greater scheme of the practical uses of law". "The functional task of adjudicative activity, in the ordinary case, is a matter of settling a legal conflict, that is, authoritatively to determine – in response, say, to the filing of a legal petition – whether an instance of human behaviour is illegal or legal."

b) Thus, we see that Brusiin uses the concept of practical uses of law in a very broad sense, encompassing very "divergent forms of activity". His cognitive interests are directed not only to jurists but also to nonjurists insofar as they are engaged, in the everyday life of the law, in practical uses of law, that is to say, are active in legal matters. And these activities, too – understood as norm-oriented action – which in one form or another serve the practical uses of law, are not presupposed as being already familiar in the customary way. Independently of the conventional tradition of legal thinking, they must first be described empirically and must be examined and clarified from the standpoint of legal theory.

2. As far as the concept of "objectification" is concerned, it arises from the relation of human history, society, and law, as understood by Brusiin. In his view, an ongoing "objectifying" of law is found in every legal community. It is an expression of the "fact" that the human being – and only the human being – has a "history" and, in particular, "that he is continually occupied in, as it were, 'co-creating' this history".

a) Here – a noteworthy point – Brusiin speaks not of general history *qua* antiquarian material but of human history *qua* "ongoing process of the organization" of the society that "continues from one century to the next". In this process "material and intellectual culture" "objectifies" itself through "the indefatigable creative work of man", understood here, too, as a social species. The law, too, belongs to this material and intellectual culture. "The law also appears in the form of a objectification, made up of many different, separately formed elements". For Brusiin, the law, understood *both* in terms of "practical uses" *and* as an expression of "legal thinking", becomes "empirically" comprehensible only by means of its "objectifications", that is to say, by means of the "products" of the process of juristic thinking, which in this way becomes accessible to experience and observation. "This objectification is something visible and audible."

b) All the presuppositions and implications of the things we create – tools, beliefs, art, our convictions, or the law – are to be seen in the meaning and sense that human beings themselves bestow upon them in a historico-social process and not in something that lies beyond them. The qualities of the socio-cultural world have no existence independently of us. Here Brusiin comes very close to the institutional theories of law as represented in connection with North American legal realism and the sociological jurisprudence of Llewellyn, Underhill Moore, Callahan and others. However, this influence of sociological jurisprudence and North American legal realism should not be overestimated.

c) In Brusiin's own case, it is a matter above all of linguistic "objectifications" in which the law appears, and of the practical uses of law in virtue of which it objectifies itself. He thinks above all of "written objectifications", for example, "statutory texts, judicial opinions, written administrative decisions, and deeds and other writings drafted by attorneys." There is no doubt that the "sense of objectifications", precisely because it bears the imprint of culture and society, can "only be disclosed through interpretation". Thus, Brusiin's theory and sociology of law acquires the character of an interpretive theory,[7] which has been current since Ihering, Max Weber and Anthony Giddens.

---

[7] See *Werner Krawietz,* "Juridisch-institutionelle Rationalität des Rechts versus Rationalität der Wissenschaften? Zur Konkurrenz divergierender Rationalitäts-

3. If all law, or at any rate modern law, is a product of "juristic thinking", which is set down in legal objectifications, then one can aim at still another advance through research in legal theory, made possible through "introspection" basing itself on personal legal experience and (self-) observation and accompanying all practical uses of law.

a) In his theory of law Brusiin takes as his point of departure the "empirical fact" that "there exists, in modern cultural states, juristic thinking". He treats it, however, not as something already familiar from its structure and function, but as something requiring empirical "research". In conducting research on juristic thinking, the researcher, in so far as he is himself "a lawyer", can "draw on his own personal experience *qua* lawyer". Therefore, he will want, for example, "to analyze the *behaviour* of the practicing attorney, whose thinking in this connection is implicitly presupposed". It is a matter of "understanding juristic thinking" as it in fact unfolds, from its own presuppositions, in order to describe and explain its characteristic moves.

b) As far as legal thinking is concerned, Brusiin makes a sharp distinction between "legal thinking" in a broad sense and "juristic thinking". The former, legal thinking, is always "thought which takes the existence of a legal system as its point of departure and which then refers all objects of thought to this legal system". Contrariwise, the latter, juristic thinking, is a special form of legal thinking, namely, "a lawyer's thinking in connection with the practical uses of law". In order to turn the process of juristic thinking "in and of itself into the object of an effective programme of scientific research", Brusiin *qua* researcher will want also to use "his own introspection", which *qua* lawyer he possesses from his familiarity with the practical uses of law. He conceives of these as a part of "personal experience in the law", which he has acquired through practical "dealings in legal situations". Entirely correctly, he remarks that in connection with various types of uses of law, "no legal researcher would want to be without his acquired personal experiences, be they directed to his own reactions or to those of colleagues in the law". Indeed, it appears appropriate to draw not only on one's own observation but also on the "observations of others' reactions", especially "observations of colleagues' uses of law".

c) Brusiin saw all too well, however, the "dangers" that "an introspective method poses". He expressly warns against introspective "speculating", regarding such as a "rudiment stemming from legal philosophy". In that he determines juristic thinking only "in connection with the practi-

---

konzepte in der modernen Rechtstheorie", RECHTSTHEORIE 15 (1984), 423 - 452, at 426f.

cal uses of law", it becomes impossible to distinguish "types of practical uses in law" that serve at the same time to characterize everyday legal thought. Therefore, Brusiin answers unhesitatingly in the affirmative the question whether an "introspective observation of one's own juristic thinking is possible". Decisive in this connection, however, is the presupposition that "the actor observes himself and his thinking as they are seen, so to speak, from without, that is, externally". The theory of law must turn the law and legal thinking into the objects of a form of inquiry taken up "from without". This condition is fulfilled if one proceeds from the practical uses of law and their objectification.

4. Perhaps we would prefer, today, to speak here of various forms and types of practical juristic argumentation. However, it is a matter not of logical forms of thinking but of regulated social forms of action through legal norms. Otto Brusiin understands the types of practical uses of law that he worked up as "ideal types" in Max Weber's sense and which underlie his juridico-theoretical analysis. He saw all too well that one can raise objections to the "use of ideal types" on the ground that "they cannot be squared with strictly empirical research". Still, to him it appeared that their use was justified on the ground that these ideal types – looking to the practical uses of law – are suited to serve in clarifying the empirical connections between norms and action.

5. Like many truly original legal thinkers who opened up new vistas and acquired new insights in their efforts to understand the cognition of law, Otto Brusiin did not provide a complete, closed, and conceptually systematic representation of his theory of law. However, the partial insights that he acquired, supported and secured through experience and observation, stand in an inner and genuinely systematic connection to each other. This connection requires a representation in an altogether renewed external system, which brings the totality of the new insights he has worked up into a mosaic. He left this task – perhaps a lesser task – to the succeeding generation. But even without these *desiderata* of theory reconstruction, Brusiin's work *Man and His Law* shows that he is rightly to be numbered among the greatest European legal thinkers of our century, this thanks to the new basis of modern legal theory set out by him there, even if not set out by him alone.

Owing to limitations of space, I cannot offer here a reconstruction of Brusiin's legal theory. I am concerned alone with the essential insights and guidelines he offers for future work in legal theory, which – though contained in his work – have not yet been fully received and assimilated. In what follows I would therefore like to concentrate on three questions: (1) What was and is really new in Brusiin's legal theory? (2) Which misunderstandings, occurring in fact or simply possible, might lead to a distorted or inadequate characterization of his legal theory? (3) Which of the problems in legal theory already pointed out by Brusiin remain unresolved even today or have been insufficiently dealt with? Answering these three questions promises at the same time to shed more light on, and to add some particulars to, the evaluation of Brusiin's theory of law.

IV. What is New in Brusiin's Theory of Law?

1. In Otto Brusiin's self-image we find from the beginning a very clearly developed consciousness of the novelty, and also the boldness, of his approach to legal theory. "In the history of the sciences", so he remarked in 1947, "one ascertained that a new science begins to emancipate itself from the queen mother philosophy as soon as the conditions for its own existence are given". Brusiin followed up on this remark with his own diagnosis and therapeutic suggestion: "At this point in time, legal theory finds itself in this emancipatory phase. And it can develop into a fruitful science only as an independent discipline, one that does justice to its own internal demands."

a) The discipline Brusiin asked for and that established itself on a new basis quite consciously sets itself apart from the traditional philosophico-moral or philosophico-juridical theories of principles and from the encyclopedic representations of the law familiar from the nineteenth century. Legal theory no longer has as its aim to be "merely a form of encyclopedia", that is, a "herbarium pieced together from some general concepts of legal expertise". Legal theory separates itself consciously in its method and in its systematic access to law from all of these predecessors.

b) Brusiin's theory of law, however, also separates itself quite consciously from the connection to all earlier forms of "legal philosophy". This is true, above all, for the case of philosophical idealism, especially idealistic legal and social philosophy. It is also the case, however, for older natural law thinking and its metaphysical presuppositions and implications, which cannot withstand the critique of epistemology and the philosophy of science. That its mode of proceeding also has philosophical presuppositions and implications is not overlooked by Brusiin; it is, however, a different chapter in the inquiry into his work.

c) As a title for this new legal theory, separated from the traditional philosophies, Brusiin came up with "general legal theory" – perhaps somewhat misleading in the context of German legal thought. "Seen purely linguistically", he wrote, *"Rechtstheorie"* would be the "best term", but he feared that this designation would be mixed up with the term "legal science", already well established. Later, in 1951, in his book

"On Everyday Legal Thought", he tells us he had serious reservations about the use of the term *"Allgemeine Rechtslehre"*, which he had used up until then – and once again the reservations stemmed from his concern over the danger of the mix up. Instead, he now suggested that the term *"Allgemeine Rechtstheorie"* be used. And, in a line addressed to the German public in legal science, he writes: "Would it not lie in the interest of a unified international terminology in this field if the term *'Allgemeine Rechtstheorie'* were also introduced into academic German?"

2. What was and is really new in the legal thought of Brusiin? That is something – what with the knowledge *of* the law and *about* the law that is available to us today – that one can recognize far more easily today than would have been possible at the end of the 1940's or at the beginning of the 1950's. This period, as I see it, was the really original and at the same time most fruitful and creative period of all of Brusiin's work. The effects of his work from this period impart to modern legal theory even today genuinely significant initiatives and impulses. During the 1960's and the beginning of the 1970's, a period during which important consequences of his new approach to legal thought were drawn out, his own work was devoted more to securing and working out still further the contributions of the earlier period – to be sure, always with an eye to the bases of all law as he had diagnosed them. In this connection I am not overlooking the fact that Brusiin – beginning with his dissertation on "The Discretion of the Judge in Cases of Gaps in the Law" – had also dealt with the positive law over his entire academic career and that he had had a hand in the positive law in a great variety of different ways, as is evident from his publications. Drawing on this background, he distinguished various steps in the "objectifying" of the law, that is, various forms of social formation of law as well as various levels of legal thinking. They also opened up various different possibilities of theoretical access to the law. I might then turn to a brief sketch of these levels, for they are characteristic of the legal thinking of Brusiin. The individual levels of his legal thinking, which collectively make possible both a more differentiated access to the law and a profound knowledge of its own character, are distinguished in the degree of abstraction and in their distance from the respective contentual problems of the practical uses of law, without however losing, not to mention ignoring, the standing orientation to these reference points – the case, unfortunately, with many "modern" and "post-modern" approaches to legal thought.

a) At level 1, it is a matter of the "objectifying of law", that is, of legal practice itself and of the practical "uses of law" that are bound up with it in the situations of everyday life. Legal practice "objectifies" itself, however, not only in the practical legal activity of decisionmaking, that is, in legal actión, but also and above all in the language of the prevailing law. The latter is at the same time the medium with whose help legal practice and the legal thinking bound up with it engage, as it were, in self-reflection. Indeed, what is true of this situation was given effective expression by Ilmar Tamelo[8] in Salzburg on the occasion of a Finnish-Austrian symposium on legal theory in 1980: "Law is a reflexive phenomenon that relates to itself." Brusiin, however, had never rested content with a merely reflexive jurisprudence, and he never reduced his legal theory to a mere science of reflection, which would almost of necessity have distorted the peculiarly social character of the law – and this for reasons that Brusiin himself addresses.

b) At level 2, it is a matter of "legal dogmatics", that is, a matter of practical (dogmatic) legal science, which deals with the law and its interpretation "in systematic form". Whether dogmatic legal science is in need of the modern legal theory postulated and conceived by Brusiin is a question that remains controversial even today, a question that must strike one who has not dealt with legal theory as difficult.[9] We recall that nineteenth-century economic theory first had to overcome certain growing pains before it emerged as a success.

c) At level 3, we are concerned with the doctrine of juristic method, which, in turn, is a matter of the method of practical uses of law and dogmatic legal science, that is, the traditional "method of jurisprudence". The term and the concept *"jurisprudence"* are not to be interpreted here in the sense of the Anglo-Saxon term "Jurisprudence", which is best translated by the German *"Allgemeine Rechtslehre"* ("general legal theory"). Rather, *"jurisprudence"* is understood here in the traditional sense of *"iuris prudentia"*, that is to say, a practical technique for coming to terms with legal texts. It is at the same time the "method of legal thinking" and concerns above all – in part found in practical uses of law, in part set up by itself – rules of the "correct" application of law.

d) It is only at level 4, that is, at a relatively high degree of desistance, abstraction and generality of the hypotheses set out and of the legal experiences acquired and examined with their help, that a general theory of law – or, better, a legal theory, set out on a new basis by Brusiin – emerges. In what follows I will be dealing with level 4 alone, although Brusiin leaves no doubt that his legal theory in a fully devel-

---

8 See *Krawietz,* "Zur Struktur von Entwicklung und Fortschritt in der Rechtstheorie" (note 2), at 344 f.

9 See *Werner Krawietz,* Juristische Entscheidung und wissenschaftliche Erkenntnis. Eine Untersuchung zum Verhältnis von dogmatischer Rechtswissenschaft und rechtswissenschaftlicher Grundlagenforschung (Vienna & New York 1978).

oped form would also produce significant effects on levels 1 - 3. This is certainly correct. I am also not overlooking the fact that Brusiin in his many-sided collective works has made significant contributions, through his own legal thought, to all these levels. I am not here concerned, however, to work out the novelty of his theory of law. In it he succeeds in giving expression to a paradigm shift within the theory of law – and here Thomas Kuhn's sometimes misused expression of the "paradigm shift" is altogether appropriate. And even that is new and, indeed, revolutionary in legal theory and legal philosophy, which until now – without prejudice to hermeneutical access to the law – had never so consistently and resolutely brought into the foreground the experiential and observational relation between legal norms and action and also considered both as historico-societal products of their time – never before, with the exception of Ihering and Max Weber, and, independently of course, Hegel and Marx, even if Brusiin in an altogether characteristic way puts considerable distance between himself and these last two.

3. The novelty of Brusiin's legal thought is to be seen above all in the fact that he conceived and developed his theory of law through a radical break with the tradition in European legal thought. He breaks with the traditional ideal of the unity of theory and practice, which determined the relation between legal practice and legal science in various legal cultures over centuries. The traditional view, from which Brusiin turns away, is given expression in an exemplary and prominent form by the Swiss writer Walter Burckhardt[10] in his famous work Method and System of the Law, when he writes: "The task of science cannot be separated from practice, that is, from the task of those who issue and apply the law." With this view, prevailing to the present day in European jurisprudence and understood here as *iuris prudentia,* Brusiin contrasts his own view, which stands diametrically opposed to the prevailing view: "A clear, principal separation must be made between everyday legal thinking, that is, the thought of the practicing attorney vis-à-vis practical uses of law, and the thought of jurisprudence, that is, scientific research into questions legal in nature."

a) One could scarcely have drawn a sharper separation within legal thought, until then conceived of as a unity. Brusiin gives expression to exactly this separation when he defines "everyday legal thought", understood as the "thought of the lawyer vis-à-vis the practical uses of law", in such a way that "scientific" legal thinking, especially that of the legal scientist who works and teaches at a university, "does not fall thereunder". This "principal distinction" has as a consequence the fact that

---

10 Cited from *Brusiin,* Der Mensch und sein Recht (note 3), at 225.

the collective legal thinking on levels 1 - 3, because of its dominating tie to and association with "everyday legal thinking", must now first be carried over into the sphere of research in legal theory.

b) Rendered suspect for want of genuine scientific character, everyday legal thinking and action are now turned into an object of "empirical" research, which proceeds descriptively and seeks to describe, to clarify, and to explain its newly determined object. Brusiin's scientific and cognitive programme is a "theory of law" that is conceptualized and based sociologically.

c) If one asks about the intellectual origins and predecessors of the sociological turn in his legal thought, these would be sought – if I understand Brusiin correctly – above all in Ihering and Roscoe Pound (and, if you will, also in Marx, from whom Brusiin to be sure clearly disassociates himself). These intellectual origins are found, however, above all in Max Weber, on whose theory and sociology of law, and ideal-typical method Brusiin builds. And indeed, Brusiin acted upon his original and genuinely juridico-theoretic scientific programme at once, as above all *Man and His Law* now shows.

That which is new in Brusiin's legal thought discloses itself to us, however, only if we ask: With the help of which distinctions, forms, and categories did Brusiin observe the social reality of the law? In writing this paper I have often inquired into the price that Brusiin as jurist and as university professor had to pay, possibly in the various forums of legal practice and in legal science, for his novel insights into the structure and function of all law. Was his price merely the loneliness of one who opened up new ways? One does not violate the unwritten rule of a profession that is centuries old without paying a penalty, not even if one enjoys its privileges as a university teacher of law.

4. I am not in a position to judge how Brusiin's "theory of law" was received in Finland. However, I can and would like to offer from my own experience a small facet respecting its effects internationally. Let me begin in this connection by relating a short anecdote.

a) Although I never met Otto Brusiin personally, I remember well my first contact with his legal theory. It took place in the year 1958, that is, nearly 40 years ago. I had just passed my first state examination in law and on the very next day had decided to begin work on a dissertation. I knew very well what the theme of the doctoral dissertation was going to be: "The positive law and its function". I had just completed a double course of study – both law and economics. It was above all the latter that influenced my choice of dissertation themes. Since the economic sciences – understood as economics and business or management –

describe and explain, in economic theory, one and the same economic system, I wanted to investigate from the standpoint of legal science the legal system and, with it, all legally regulated human behaviour. As a jurist, I was trained – as was then and is, still today, usually the case – only at levels 1 and 2, but I was well-versed in theory formation in economics, thanks to my second field of study. I therefore assumed as something altogether obvious that in the mountains of writing devoted to legal thought, there had to exist a legal theory – comparable to economic theory – that stood in need of further development. I therefore did not understand my doctoral supervisor, who had gladly accepted me and clearly wanted what was best for me but did not share my enthusiasm for the theme at all, advising me that the matter ought to be reconsidered. Owing to the normativity of all law, a matter with which I was conversant at levels 1 and 2, I was not worried. That is, the task of explaining the connection between norms and human action from the standpoint of legal theory did not appear to me to be a barrier at all.

aa) The following may show you how naively, methodologically and juridico-theoretically, I then proceeded: I set for myself a period of three months, during which time I would gather together and examine all the relevant writings; it was in this connection that I experienced the greatest disappointment and defeat of my life. To be sure, I found a great many books in legal method, in general legal theory (here understood as the theory of principles) and in every variety of legal philosophy, but – apart from Kelsen, who appeared to this German jurist far too devoted to the state, and too closely bound to statutory and legal positivism – I found nothing that, either in subject matter or methodology, would have satisfied the cognitive and scientific standards familiar to me from economic theory.

bb) This situation only changed when, in the library of the Institute for Public Law and Politics, I stumbled onto two works of a Finnish author by the name of Otto Brusiin, then unknown to me. The works in question were entitled "On Adjudication" and "On Legal Thinking". I had to recognize that *the* theory, the one I had had in mind and had sought, did not exist. With Brusiin's help, however, I was able to recognize why this was so. What is more, he pointed out the direction in which one had to travel in order to correct the problem, and he had already traveled a good distance in this direction himself. It was not difficult for me to follow him, for in my own German legal system I was able to make some of the very observations and insights that he had described in his structural analysis of the law.

cc) I experience some years later the second great disappointment vis-à-vis the standards that Brusiin had set down and that I had accepted; it was in 1967, at the World Congress of the International Association for Philosophy of Law and Social Philosophy (IVR) in Gardone Riviera. This was the first World Congress that I ever attended, having in the meantime become active in the field as a researcher. The theme of the Congress was "'Is' and 'Ought' in the Field of Legal Experience". It was – judged on the basis of what had been promised – a true flop. For it had become nothing more than a Kelsen-Congress, which, therefore, had nothing to do with experience and observation in the field of law and which was thus not in a position to reach to questions of the social reality of law.

b) This disappointment was the occasion for a decision that I took together with two colleagues – meeting outside the Congress hall – to establish a journal for "legal theory" that would provide an outlet for new and novel efforts in the field. In connection with the programme and the title of the journal, which mentioned in its sub-title "logic, theory of method, cybernetics, and legal sociology", Otto Brusiin had served as godfather, albeit without knowing it! In the conversation with the publisher, the unforgettable Johannes Broermann, over the founding of the journal – a conversation that took place soon after the initial meeting and which lasted some five hours – the question of what, in such a journal, would be new was the main topic of discussion. Insofar as my participation in the founding of the journal was concerned, the answers to these questions were not difficult. My answers, and supporting arguments too, which I made my own, can be read today in *Man and His Law*. In 1970 – some twenty years after the suggestion made by Brusiin – the new journal appeared under the name he had preferred, namely RECHTSTHEORIE.

It was only after the meeting, indeed, much later, that it became clear to me how very much in my own legal thinking I owed, from the beginning, to the legal thought of Otto Brusiin. Since then we have all reaped a great deal from him and have passed on to an international readership much of what he and many others have sown. I am therefore happy to express – also vis-à-vis his relatives, especially his wife, Professor Dr. Hilkka Brusiin, and his daughter, Frau Kaarina Suonio, former Minister of Research and today the mayor of Tampere – the great gratitude that I feel in recalling Otto Brusiin and his work.

5. The significance of Brusiin's legal thought may lie in the fact that after the War, faced with the necessity of making a new beginning, he unlike other legal thinkers lapsed neither into a restoration of natural law thinking nor into the uncritical historical stage of statutory positivism and legal positivism, a stage that, so to speak, had simply been "interrupted" and could now be resumed. He also did not fall into the mistake of supposing that the experiences with the illegal state of the

Third Reich, an unfathomably wicked system, were simply to be traced to, as it were, an "industrial accident". In the upheaval after the Second World War, after a catastrophe that shook at any rate the European world to its foundations and, with it, the legal world of Germany and of Finland, Brusiin questioned not only norms and their content but also their causes, the motives giving rise to them, and their effects. Drawing upon himself and his own experience and observation, Otto Brusiin set out upon a lonely search for the social reality of law.

a) In Brusiin's view, the point of departure and basis of legal theory for the researcher using it are, therefore, always the "personal legal experience" of all those who are, or were, dealing with the law, including the "personal legal experience" of the researcher himself. And the legal theorist, too – whether he "becomes aware of it or not" – "always takes as his point of departure his own positive law". Notwithstanding the normativity of the positive law, the legal theorist, dealing with human action that is "rule governed" by positive law, is always occupied with observable "structural questions". Formulated in other words, one could say, too, that legal theory has to be occupied with the law as institutional fact, set normatively for the long term.

b) However, structural questions of law are, for Brusiin, generally questions about current and past social structures of the law. In that the researcher considers the positive law and its normative regulations in a temporal perspective, his research – as we have known since Ihering and Max Weber – must necessarily assume the form of a historico-societal theory of law, since all law, as Brusiin remarks, follows an "ongoing organizational process, continuing on from one century to the next". This aspect, which seeks to take account of the "collective social situation" and which brings the "entire legal system" into consideration, and from which the take-off into the future is launched, is for Brusiin a "sociological" aspect. If one proceeds to concrete examples, whose normative presuppositions are drawn from a certain legal system, one enters the field of "historico-cultural consideration", which analyzes "juristic thinking" in various concrete cultural epochs from, so to speak, the outside. Brusiin never paid homage to a cognitivism with reference to any particular legal content. With reference to the content of "social norms", especially legal norms and "values", as well as to the base-ideology of a legal system – he speaks here of "the last presuppositions of juristic thinking", which he treats at the same time as a "historico-cultural", social "fact" that stands in need of scientific explanation – Brusiin always represented a strict non-cognitivism.

c) But also in the last phase in Brusiin's legal theory, in which he appeared to retreat back into Finnish intellectual history and the background of its reception, there was no wavering from the chosen course in legal theory. Armed with juridico-theoretically integrated knowledge about the legal system of today, recovered from diverse disciplines, Brusiin looked to the past of Finnish legal culture for normatively relevant practical "decisional situations", "cases" and "rules", which, with an eye to a juridico-theoretical critique, he identified as legally significant. Obviously that does *not* mean that history "proves" what is "correct" and "good". History serves in his view only as the deliverer, so to speak, of raw legal material, on whose treatment or processing the "objectivity" of legal science and the correctness of its theory of law must prove itself. Thus, for Brusiin, the history of the law and the history of legal thought are an object of juridico-theoretical research directed to "objectified" legal norms and compliance therewith, belonging to the past. Here it is a matter of nothing other than past "legal experience". All legal experience requires a critical working out, even if long since relegated to history. For Brusiin, therefore, the history of law and the history of legal thought are nothing other than juridico-theoretical research on past norms and compliance with them. Research of this nature can and must – wherever it is possible – be carried out, moving backwards from yesterday all the way to the beginnings of human society. As once formulated by Franz Wieacker: the concern is with that "extract of the past" in which one can meet with human experience of law.

V. Opponents of Brusiin's Legal Theory – An Unholy Alliance of Idealism, Ontologism, and Sociologism

Before I come, in closing, to a summary evaluation of Brusiin's legal theory, I should like at any rate to mention three possible misunderstandings of his "theory of law". The objections in question here are raised against all merely "empirical" legal theories, usually by those who in their own theoretical approach do not want to orient themselves, at least not primarily, to the "social reality of law". They satisfy themselves with a polemical neutralization of competing views, in order – undisturbed by the formation of a legal realist or sociological theory of law – to be able to carry on just as before. I mean the three unholy sisters – or, illuminated by feminism, should I say "brothers"? – who in connection with such polemical suspicions form an almost familial unity, namely, the charges of (i) *idealism,* of (ii) *ontologism,* and of (iii) *sociologism* in legal thinking.

1. In German, easily misunderstood expressions such as the "objectifying of law", "objectivity of adjudication", and the "objectivity of the sciences", or even formulations such as "the connection between the

objectivity of science and the objectivity of law" can give rise to the impression – a false impression, to be sure – of a Hegelian-like mode of speech and thus, an idealistic approach to law. Also, many readers of Brusiin may well be inclined to place Brusiin's legal theory somewhere between idealism and realism, which would be equally false. Brusiin's theory of law has nothing in common with philosophical idealism; rather, it is the successful effort, from the standpoint of legal theory, to overcome idealism. Brusiin is also no proponent of legal realism, another claim that is easily made. And in the conceptualization of his legal theory, he is not at all subject to the dangers of conceptual realism, dangers that were familiar to him from his methodological reflections. This becomes clear at the latest if one distinguishes, with Brusiin, (1.) between philosophical realism and legal realism, and, insofar as the latter is concerned, (2.) takes up what is, indeed, an indispensable distinction between Scandinavian and North American legal realism.

a) If Brusiin were labeled a "realist" at all, then, owing to the misleading connotations of philosophical realism that should if at all possible be avoided, he was a legal realist in the sense of sociological jurisprudence and American legal realism, which deals with the connections between norms and action, that is, between legal norms and legal action where the norms in question exist in fact and are efficacious. To be sure, I believe that this would amount to a half-truth, for Brusiin in my judgment builds on the foundations of sociological jurisprudence and German legal realism from Ihering to Max Weber, which have understood all law with reference to human action as a normatively efficacious social structure. In contrast to many proponents of American legal realism, Brusiin seeks in his theory and sociology of law to avoid the leveling of the normative. On the other hand, he criticizes with good reason Kelsen's one-sided "pure" normativism; Kelsen – as Brusiin puts it – sketched a "picture of the law as a sphere of the 'ought' separated from the 'is'", a picture "omitting" that which is "central", namely "human action". With respect to human action, it appeared to Brusiin to be a "fruitful idea" "to secure to human action a fitting position within legal theory", which he succeeded in doing with the help of his own legal theory.

b) In that Brusiin sets every "legal situation giving rise to concrete uses of law against the potential background of the entire legal system" as it in fact exists and is efficacious, both experientially and observably, he is in a position in his legal theory of the "world of juristic thinking and action" to sketch a socially adequate conception and reconstruction, a theory that seeks at the same time to do justice to all human experience and action. His reformulation orients itself from the beginning on the social reality of law and on its practical political functions; hence, it serves human orientation in action both in a factual and in a normative respect. The reformulation is also in a position – and this is important for the analysis of modern information and communication systems of law – to show that every merely halfways "unified mass steering of human behaviour" is not only politically but also juridico-practically a "thoroughly difficult task". It sets lay persons as well as jurists in connection with practical uses of law "continually before new situations for whose mastery one has no complete scheme".

2. To understand Brusiin's legal theory as a form of legal ontology, or, insofar as its philosophical bases are concerned, to suspect it of ontologism, would also appear to me to be mistaken. This interpretation would be inappropriate for the reason, first of all, that Brusiin in his "theory of law" nowhere uses an "ontic" or "ontological" mode of speech; he observes without exception an epistemic and genuinely juridico-theoretical approach to the law, in which he takes as his point of departure – in an ideal-typical interpretive method – the experiences and observations of "practical uses of law". His legal theory is also far removed from every form of "rule platonism" and from every normative ontology of the social. He is also no representative of an ontological holism, which – always presupposing in an untested way the whole of the legal system and the society as putatively authoritative but as in the end impenetrable – always simply talks about these entities instead of actually investigating them.

a) As far as the relation between anthropology and ontology is concerned, it would be little short of absurd to suspect Brusiin of ontologism. I would therefore also not wish to characterize his "theory of law" as a form of legal anthropology, based on a philosophical anthropology. On the contrary, Brusiin distinguishes between "philosophical speculation" – especially "metaphysics" and "scientific research" – and he has put every form of "philosophical anthropology" behind him. He would, at best, have been ready to replace "philosophical" anthropology with a "scientific" anthropology, whose non-existence was something Brusiin had to diagnose. Since Brusiin in the upheaval after the Second World War took leave of classical, metaphysico-speculative legal and social philosophy, the turn to the social reality of the law became not only possible but, indeed, indispensable.

The insights of anthropology, systemically heterogeneous vis-à-vis the various standing disciplines, which are drawn out in connection with the grounding of his own legal theory, have only the function of pointing out that, so to speak, a finely detailed, "firm" and ontologically clear "nature of man" cannot be specified at all. Thus, the human individual, too, seen as a putatively last and holistically understood entity, is displaced from theory formation.

b) Brusiin's "theory of law" makes clear that, and why, the human being *qua* living creature, whose social behaviour is not fixed but is thoroughly open to its environment, is dependent on the creation, preservation and security of self-produced social action and guidance systems, in whose framework all autonomous human experience and action – prestructured by means of "social norms", especially legal norms – are developed and realized in ordered forms of life. In this regard norms are "specific or peculiar to the human being, and are conditioned by means of his co-existence in societies", but they contain only "schemes for action directed to the future, which – by contrast to instinctive patterns – are in principle changeable". The "setting up of abstract schemes of action, according to which concrete human acts can be judged and coercive sanctions imposed", is therefore only a "rationalizing technique of the law" – nothing less, but also nothing more.

c) Brusiin does not overlook the obvious fact that one can, may, and indeed must also – secondarily – question the ontological, epistemological and other philosophical presuppositions of all law. In his view, however, the work of those sciences that deal with the law – in whatever form – must be carried out first; only then can legal theory integrate their insights. To that extent – but also only to that extent – there would still remain room for a secondary "ontology of norms" of a new form, which is, however, yet to be created. With this, however, legal and social philosophy are brought to a position that appears to be subordinate to that of the sciences concerned with human experience and action. Philosophy thus thrives by drawing on the premises of those disciplines that deal with the relation between legal norms and action.

3. It is no wonder, then, that this conception of legal theory brought down on Brusiin's head the reproach of the "sociologizing of legal sciences", formulated most prominently by Carlos Cossio. It reached its apex in the charge that Brusiin in his legal thinking had fallen victim to "sociologism".[11] Both charges are altogether mistaken.

a) In Brusiin's case, one certainly must speak of an effort to explain jurisprudence and its tasks largely or, indeed, exclusively in sociological terms. For in his analysis of the relation of norms and action he differentiates very carefully and pleads for a cautious, and in this form certainly altogether appropriate, consideration of social relations and conditions. Naturally, in reference to legal theory there is no question of sociologism in the sense of the tendency to explain all intellectual and

11 *Brusiin,* Der Mensch und sein Recht (note 3), 202 f.

cultural facts and the factors determining them exclusively as societal conditions and to interpret them only sociologically.

b) It is not least of all for this reason that Brusiin postulated and established legal theory as an independent discipline, relying on inter- and multi-disciplinary cooperation with many other sciences, for he knew that for the description, clarification, and explanation of the social connections existing between norms and action, no one of the many sciences that would come into consideration is competent by itself – not legal science either and certainly not sociology. It speaks on behalf of the scientific noblesse manifested in Brusiin's critical exchanges with opponents that in his replies – soliciting, so to speak, understanding for Cossio – he asks the reader only to consider "that the boundary between legal sociology and a theory of law conceptualized in the spirit of sociology is not very sharp". It is a mark of the worth of his "theory of law" that Brusiin masterfully drew this distinction and used it.

4. If one takes as the point of departure the fact that the polemical objections and conjectures mentioned above offer a distorted picture of Brusiin's legal theory, it appears that the widespread need for a short and concise characteristic that would serve as a shorthand description of his theory of law in relation to other theory formations that compete with it, is, while thoroughly understandable, not only difficult but, indeed, without very careful analyses not forthcoming at all. Many critics might, however, be tempted to replace the three "isms", deemed not suitable for characterizing Brusiin's legal theory, with a critical *Topos*. The critics would then be claiming that Brusiin's "theory of law" has fallen victim to holism. For in its analysis of "juristic thinking" the "entire legal system" always forms the potential backdrop. This objection, too, which is popular in the critique of analyses of collective societies, I regard as mistaken. The charge of holism is mistaken for the reason that Brusiin carefully distinguishes among (i) interactional, (ii) organizational, and (iii) societal connections of all legal experience and action. He has also been concerned to conduct research on (iv) the reciprocal interactions that exist between these connections instead of simply presupposing them without having subjected them to test. Moreover, he understands (v) neither *the* individual nor *the* society as final entities or wholes, which as such cannot be further questioned and analyzed. One can see, therefore, in Brusiin's theoretical access to law – access that turns on the normatively efficacious structure of all social relations, relations to which the law, too, is a party – a genuine juridico-theoretical alternative both to individualism and to a societal holism as well as an alternative to a moral and socio-theoretical universalism and holism.

a) In the conception of his legal theory Brusiin has never fallen into the individualistic misunderstanding that the society exists basically only in individuals or in groups of individuals. Against this view of juridico-philosophical and moral individualism, according to which all law is simply a result of the properties and decisions of individuals, that is, results from the unified and expressed will of the assembly of such individuals or of their formations in groups, and in this way serves as a universal means toward bringing about a binding order, Brusiin juxtaposes his view of the historico-social character of the legal system.

aa) According to Brusiin's view, all law – in reference to all members who are included in the normative system of a legal community, who are, indeed, ordinarily born into this community – is always found at a higher socio-structural level than are all concrete individuals or their formations in groups, whose behaviour is regulated on the basis of and according to the standards of this legal system. Therefore one cannot determine, describe, interpret or explain the law as a normative, emergent social structure by taking – and this also by means of merely analytico-theoretical tools – principally the unbound individuals as one's point of departure, without having already determined the emergent properties of the legal system itself. The legal system as a whole is and remains as such a subsystem of the society. Precisely here lies the central insight of Brusiin's legal theory, which he shares with the representatives of German legal realism and sociological jurisprudence, the sociological institutional theory of law, and systems theory. Thus, it is simply not the case that all law can be understood as, so to speak, a subsequently imposed limitation of and restriction on those individuals and formations of groups affected by law, which are *a priori* not limited but are absolutely "free". Rather, the law – following the encoding through the legal system, which has the capacity of characterizing all human experience and action fundamentally and generally as legal or illegal, that is, as lawful or unlawful – serves from the beginning the programming and conditioning of all actual and possible experience and action, which is, in this way, institutionally established for the long term. In virtue of this "legal schematization" set out by Brusiin with good reason as *the* social achievement of "legal thinking", the "equality of citizens before the law" can at one and the same time both be made possible and can be realized. Furthermore, through this "schematization", the legal responsibility of the individual is translated into institutionally acceptable and practical forms.

bb) Therefore the state, too, as Brusiin emphasizes, has in connection with the social organization of the legal system – in spite of the "monopoly position" claimed by it – always only to perceive a subordinate and normatively regulated, politico-legal function. For Brusiin, the state is therefore not *the* legal community, superordinate to all others, and equipped so to speak with a "monopoly" vis-à-vis law creation, but is only *one* among "the many legal communities that exist today". To these legal communities, for example, belong – considered historico-socially – also the churches and professional organizations, such as the unions, the associations of medical doctors and of attorneys, which, existing not only "within the contemporary state" as autonomous legal communities, but also internally, that is, in relation to their own members, also "formulate", concretely determine, and give effect to" their own law. Also, the alleged fact that "in most modern states the statutory law has enjoyed a position of preeminence", is, for Brusiin, who long ago dispensed with traditional statutory and legal positivism in his theory of law, "apparent rather than real". For him, "a state or a regulation in and of itself is only a celebrated announcement of a project for a new regulation", which must now become "truly effective law" and thus is and remains dependent on many "factors". Brusiin shares to that extent the view of German legal realism and German sociological jurisprudence, which in the law set by the state as such was – without prejudice to compliance with the law – only a programme of behaviour, a programme of jurisdiction, nothing more but nothing less either. In this way, therefore, through the permanent range of application of programmes of this nature the practical decisionmaking behaviour both in the everyday life of the law and in the practice of juristic decisionmaking, is in fact influenced, directed, and steered, but of course not determined dispositively.

cc) Brusiin therefore understands – without prejudice to their comprehension through legal thinking – all legal communities or, as one would more precisely formulate it today, namely, in socio-scientific terms: all in fact identifiable and observable social systems, as for example a relation of interaction between two persons who undertake a sales transaction, a family, a school, or a business, understanding them above all as genuinely social elements with emerging socio-structural properties that one can recognize and understand as such if one analyzes and interprets them on different levels in consideration of their different systemic referents. As a result, he was never able to share the love that both analytic philosophy and anglo-american idealism have had for socio-philosophical individualism, and the individualistic theory of action, which seeks to trace all human experience and action to the properties of the individual, the acting individual, that is, to trace them to *a priori* life essences informed by reason. For these approaches to thought manifest no interest in the concrete forms of interaction between human beings and also, no interest in the organized social relations accessible through experience and observational methods of analysis in the social sciences, let alone an interest in the social reality of the law, which Brusiin sought to understand within the framework of his structural theory.

b) Brusiin also did not subscribe to a societal universalism or holism, which regards the society or the legal and moral systems as ontological wholes, whose internal structure does not lend itself to in-depth analysis with the result that they remain in their fundamentals impenetrable.

aa) Instead of initially engaging in methodologically controlled social science investigations and analyses of social structure, based on experience and observation, these approaches to thought attempt in an idealistic and speculative way to tie the consideration of all law and its explanation to a preconceived ethico-theoretical reason, which with the simple principles and maxims of reason found in a reflexive universal morality is supposed to guarantee qualified or at the very least the virtual assent of all those affected, but cannot do precise this. In reality, these approaches fail owing to the observation, founded empirically, of the critical confrontation with the legal forms of life that are in fact practiced, which are, in social reality, institutionally set into place with the means of the law, and which are realized in the ongoing compliance with law as in the reproduction of the legal system.

bb) There is no sense in which Brusiin's concern is with a methodological holism in legal thinking, which would contend that through merely speculative reference to the entire legal system – understood here as a whole – the analysis of its parts or structural elements is deferred or, indeed, fully abandoned. On the contrary, Brusiin is concerned with the analysis and investigation of details, as in the analysis of the normative socio-structural elements of interactional systems and organizations, which are continually fixed on adjudication, are based on social expectations of behaviour, and at the same time become efficacious as genuinely social conditions and presuppositions. Normative expectations of behaviour of this nature function as emergent structures of all legal communication. Their distinctive character does not open up some sort of holistic intuition or merely speculatively *in mente* produced, and reasonable reflexive, balances or explanatory value of social science. They can only be researched juridico-theoretically if – as Brusiin has done – one gives up altogether the dearly won but outmoded idea of the whole or, indeed, of the totality of the society. Instead, as sketched above, the social relations between norms and human action take their place at the forefront, and their systematic and socio-structural emergent properties require more probing juridico-theoretical research.

c) With respect to concrete situations in which one sees oneself called to action, conscious of one's responsibility, Brusiin takes as his point of departure for the analyses of the relation between norm and action the idea that this relation is historically and socially conditioned and determined in a great variety of ways – and not only through the state, which issues a regulation with the means of the law. In that Brusiin in his theory and sociology of law rejects both individualism and holism, he is in a position to subject the relation of law and state to an independent judgment. His determination of this relation is characterized, above all, through the fact that he critically poses the question of the position of the state as a social construction, and he does this by analyzing from the standpoint of social and legal theory the claimed "monopoly position" of the state. He thereby arrives at the result that the state "is by no means the only legal community". Rather, the state represents itself – insofar as the state is present at all, what is by no means the case in all known forms of society – as a "passageway to higher, territorially more encompassing forms of legal community", which serves sharply to relativize its structure and its politico-legal functions.

aa) Other than for Kelsen, who in his absolutizing of normativism identifies law and state as a mere system of norms, for Brusiin such an identification appears from the beginning not only to be empirically false but also conceptually precluded. This becomes clear, above all, from the fact that Brusiin (i) speaks not of the "state" but, more generally, of a "legal community", and this, since the state, as sketched above, is only *one* among many legal communities that exist alongside each other. He also distinguishes (ii) between legal community and legal system. While the legal community is always a "collectivity of human beings", the legal system exists as a "complex of norms of a special nature", namely, legal norms, through which the acts of these human beings are "regulated". As a result, legal community and legal system cannot and must not "be identified with each other". "A collectivity of human beings and a complex of norms cannot ever be identical."

bb) It follows, for Brusiin, that there is – considered from the point of view of a theory of the evolution of law – no jump from non-legal phenomena into the circumstances of a legally regulated society. Law always grows – without prejudice to the politico-legal functions of the state, insofar as the state exists in a particular society at all, but also independently of the state – already "from the fact" that human beings "live together in societies". According to his view the law, as the "expression of the ongoing life of human beings together", arises directly and clearly from the fact that "the collective property of man, to produce norms in communal life, is bound up with the human capacity to impose form on the world". One could scarcely bring to expression this emergence of normative social structures in a more compact way than with the words of the ancient legal dictum: *ubi societas, ibi ius*.

cc) According to the view of Brusiin, all law from the very beginning therefore functions as an essential component of the normative structure of every society. However, the law is for Brusiin – in contrast to Marx – not simply a phenomenon of the superstructure. Rather, the juridico-theoretical interests of Brusiin also direct themselves (i) to the law of those societies that do not know a state in the modern sense of the word at all, as well as (ii) to the fact, very much neglected in contemporary legal theory, that in state-organized legal systems there exists alongside the state law at the same time always a non-state law, a societal law, more or less independent of the state and its decisionmaking organization. Both are profoundly shaped through the respective level of development of social institutionalization and organization, which they presuppose, and to which they are attached and to which they remain bound. According to Brusiin, the human "legal community" – as the sub-title of his book "On Legal Thinking" reads – always presupposes "the human being and his law" but *not* necessarily also the state, which as a social "organization" provides a part of those norms created by the "human society" with its "authoritative stamp of approval".

d) One cannot emphasize often enough that the distinctive character of Brusiin's access to the law consists in the fact that he sees the law, supported by his own experience and observation, above all and primarily as a social product. Indeed, this socio-theoretical basis of his approach is thoroughly characteristic of his legal thought. At the same time, it shows that with his critique on the one-sidedness of legal thought, he very early on dispensed with the juristic positivism customarily associated with legal thought – a view of the law that exhausted itself, in his lifetime, in a state-law statutory and legal positivism, but which nevertheless persists even today in a number of states of the European legal community. As is well known, this juristic positivism was not in a position, in its theory of the law – alongside the law issued or derived, or at any rate derivable by the state – even to imagine an independent societal law worthy of the name, apart from state recognition of that law. Brusiin had thought through what was for many a jurist and legal positivist the unthinkable in his presuppositions and consequences and – oriented on the experience and observation of legal practice – also brought this to expression conceptually in his theory of law. Thus, we have in his case a theory of legal pluralism, which works with a double concept of law – that is to say, not only a state concept but also a non-state concept, namely, of genuinely social law, but without any suggestion that this latter concept is deprived of its legal quality.[12] The development of

12 *Werner Krawietz,* "Der soziologische Begriff des Rechts", Rechtshistorisches Journal 7 (1988), 157 - 77, at 170ff., 174f.

modern legal ethnology and cultural anthropology is also something that Brusiin acknowledged as correct in this respect. In that he imbedded his theory of law from the beginning in a theory of the legal community, he was in a position not only to relativize the position of the nation states – no longer so prominent in the world society – but at the same time to name and to determine the historico-social legal foundations of the inter- and transnational social formations. In contrast to the case of Tönnies, who critically and polemically juxtaposed community *(Gemeinschaft)* and society *(Gesellschaft)*,[13] Brusiin saw all social formations as thoroughly products of social organization. This is true also for all legal societies.[14] How legal theory and organization theory work together here is another question. A reconstruction of Brusiin's theory of legal communities, a reconstruction that goes into detail, remains, if I am right, a *desideratum* of juridico-theoretical basic research to the present day.

VI. Possibilities and Standards of Theory Evaluation

The question whether the theory of law has to restrict itself to a normative point of view remains controversial and open right up to the present day. It is well known that Kelsen and Stammler represented the view that the specific point of view of legal theory cannot be causal but only normative. Brusiin for his part, in his critique of this view, takes as a point of departure the idea that this is only a reflection of "the dominant persuasion in traditional jurisprudence". It cannot follow, from this, "that the theory of law must also remain true to this persuasion". In that Brusiin from the beginning understands all law as a normatively efficacious structure, he is in a position to tie together normative *and* causal points of view. For "from an empirical standpoint" human action oriented to legal norms appears "just as bound, causally, as everything else". According to the functional-structural view of the law, which he shares, the "experiences of the community of mankind over a millennium" show "that it is in any case possible in certain fields to effect human behaviour decisively through statutory rules and legal decisions". This conception covers itself to a very considerable extent with the approaches to thought of a theory and sociology of law as they were represented in Germany since Ihering and in our own century by, above all, Max Weber and Helmut Schelsky. I mean to say – and with this I come to my conclusion – that one can only do justice to the greatness

---

13 See *Brusiin*, op. cit., p. 143.

14 Clearly Brusiin finds conceptual support here in Jan-Magnus Jansson; he, too, in his legal and state theory uses the expression *"rättgemenskap"*.

and the significance of Otto Brusiin's legal theory if one makes the effort to assess it in the light of the great approaches to legal theory that have steered contemporary discussion in the field. In a comparison of theories, which of course I am not able to undertake here,[15] Brusiin's theory would certainly fare well, above all, if one keeps in mind the deficits of the "great" legal theories that dominate discussion today. No one, to date, has been in a position fully to redeem the promise of the *cognitive and research programme* set up by Brusiin, a programme entirely representative for modern legal theory.

1. As far as analytico-hermeneutical legal theory is concerned, especially insofar as it is based on Wittgenstein's ordinary language philosophy,[16] it would appear to me that the efforts here are altogether compatible with the more sociologically based explanations of rule formation and rule following in Brusiin's work. Who can learn from whom? is a question that ought to be investigated more closely. We have with good reason also been taught by the philosophers that in the sphere of norms and action a normativistic point of view and a causalistic point of view can be linked together conceptually and theoretically[17] – this on the presupposition that one succeeds in developing a sufficiently differentiated theory of the framework of law,[18] with which precisely this linkage can be given effect. Also, a recent demonstration by David Bloor offers food for thought: He has shown that Wittgenstein in his later writings consistently stressed the priority of society over the individual and he regarded individual actions and convictions as cognized only within the narrow social borders of an intentional, goal-directed and planned construction and as otherwise non-intentional, so to speak, naturally evolving social phenomena.[19] This is why the concepts of "norm", "custom", "culture" and "institution" play such a prominent role in his theory. "To obey a

---

15 On this theme and on the possibilities of evaluating theories, see *Gerhard Radnitzky,* "Das Problem der Theoriebewertung", Zeitschrift für die Allgemeine Wissenschaftstheorie 10 (1979), 67 - 97, at 68f.; *Werner Krawietz,* Recht als Regelsystem (Wiesbaden 1984), at 200f.

16 See, above all, *Aulis Aarnio,* The Rational as Reasonable. A Treatise on Legal Justification (Dordrecht 1987).

17 Fundamental on this issue is *Georg Henrik von Wright,* "An Essay on Door-Knocking", RECHTSTHEORIE 19 (1988), 275 - 288; *von Wright,* "Is and Ought", in: Man, Law and Modern Forms of Life, ed. by Eugenio Bulygin et al. (Dordrecht 1985), 263 - 281, at 267f.; *von Wright,* Norm und Handlung (Königstein 1979), at 22ff., 30f., 47ff.

18 On the juridico-theoretical requirements that are to be set out vis-à-vis the construction of such a theory of the framework of law, see *Werner Krawietz,* "Identität oder Einheit des Rechtssystems?", RECHTSTHEORIE 16 (1985), at 245f., 252f., 257ff.; *Krawietz,* "Recht und moderne Systemtheorie", RECHTSTHEORIE, Beiheft 10 (1986), 281 - 309, at 290ff.

19 See *David Bloor,* Wittgenstein. A Social Theory of Knowledge (London 1983), at 24f.

rule, to make a report, to give an order, to play a game of chess", Wittgenstein said, "are *customs* (uses, institutions)." Once again it seems to me that a theory, this time analytico-hermeneutical legal theory and linguistic philosophy, could well profit from a sociological theory of law.

2. And Brusiin's "theory of law" need not shy away from comparisons with alleged or real sociological "super theories", for his theory provides important building blocks of the framework of law. While Habermas conceives of the legally authored social-life system – perhaps, as a late effect of his philosophical idealism, simply "reasonable", but therefore vis-à-vis the established social structures all the more critical – only as a "life world" worthy of projection and as a preserve, which is to be protected from the colonizing forces of "the system".[20] He does so, however, without dedicating genuinely juridico-scientific cognitive interests – in terms of "empirical" research – to the actual, legally structured social communications. For Luhmann, it is from the beginning social systems and not concrete persons or groups that hold together the social net of all legal communication,[21] whereby the law as a factor giving structure to social expectations occupies no especially prominent place.[22] By contrast, for Brusiin the relation between issuance of legal rules and compliance with rules has been at the center of his "theory of law" from the beginning. And its practical *and* theoretical relevance lies in the fact that – continually supported by the experience and observation of all "practical uses of law" – it has never lost contact with the "social reality of the law".

3. Finally, I find especially noteworthy the fact that Brusiin's legal theory has never fallen victim to the mixing up of "statutory and legal positivism" – whose persistent effects in Continental European legal thought to this day are familiar – with cognitive and scientific "positivism", which he evaluates in an altogether favorable way. Ever since the legal structure has been recognized as a product of social organization, it appears doubtful whether one can explain the law and its functioning at all if one merely looks at law and the state – even if, to be sure, this is the oft-proferred explanation. Even today – at any rate in my country and if one teaches in a law faculty – courage is called for if in one's

---

20 *Jürgen Habermas,* "Law as Medium and Law as Institution", in: Dilemmas of Law in the Welfare State, ed. by Gunther Teubner (Berlin 1986), 203 - 220, at 203f., 219f.

21 *Niklas Luhmann,* "The Self-Reproduction of Law and its Limits", in: Teubner (ed.) (note 20), 111 - 127.

22 On this issue see the critique by *Werner Krawietz,* "Legal Norms as Expectations? On Redefining the Concept of Law", in: Law, Morality, and Discursive Rationality, ed. by Aulis Aarnio/Kaarlo Tuori (Helsinki 1989), 109 - 140, at 113f., 121f., 130f.

theory one reduces and relativizes the role that the state has played in the creation of the law by pointing to the social "organization" of *all* law creation and if one seeks, accordingly, to interpret, to describe, and to explain the ongoing production and reproduction of the legal system as being, first of all, a social process. This Brusiin has clearly and unmistakably done with an eye to the currently prevailing positive law. In this sense, Brusiin's legal theory is a highly independent experientially and observationally bound and sociologically grounded "theory of law", and not a merely empirical sociology of law. Theory formation of this nature in the field of law appears today all the more necessary in light of the deficits of sociological theory formation, which are characteristic of the contemporary development of the sociology of law.[23] Accordingly, Brusiin's "theory of law", also when considered from a comparative perspective, is an important milestone in the international development of modern legal theory and it appears, too, to be pacesetting for the future.

In the very recent past, it has been our experience to witness the downfall of socialism in a number of European societies, the downfall of what is perhaps the most interesting and most important experiment of this century – this effort to steer morally or, more precisely, ethically, the state, the economy, and society. Perhaps, with this sobering experience and following Otto Brusiin, we ought to initiate an effort that draws on a flexible "practical uses of law" approach and that reflects the standard of the idea of justice transmitted by the legal system. This is not to say that one would need to, indeed that one could, forego inter- and multidisciplinary considerations of law creation. In Brusiin's view there remains, for legal theory, the task of further "rationalization" and a critical examination of the law as well as of legal thinking.

23 On this issue see the valuable critique of *Alberto Febbrajo,* "Sociology of Law or Sociologies of Law?", in: Developing Sociology of Law. A World-Wide Documentary Enquiry, ed. by Vincenzo Ferrari (Milan 1990), 899 - 910, at 905 ff., 909 f.

RECHTSTHEORIE 28 (1997), S. 203 - 217
Duncker & Humblot, 12165 Berlin

LEGAL SECURITY AND EQUITY

By Ernesto Garzón Valdés, Mainz

Some thirty years ago, I exchanged the first letters with Otto Brusiin. At that time, my interest was to publish a Spanish version of his *Über die Objektivität der Rechtsprechung (On the Objectivity of Jurisdiction)* in a collection of papers on social and legal philosophy edited by the National University of Córdoba (Argentina). In 1964, I translated the paper, which was published two years later. Later on, I used it in lectures and seminars. This year, when I began to prepare this lecture, I reread the text, as well as Brusiin's *Über das juristische Denken (On Legal Thinking)*. This time, I looked at these writings from the perspective of political philosophy, and more precisely from the point of view of the arguments that have been advanced to justify the state. In fact, I did find some ideas in Otto Brusiin which, in my opinion, need to be restated in order to gain plausibility, and a number of others which basically coincide with my own views, at least with respect to their points of departure. In what follows, I would like to comment on both of these sets of ideas. First of all, it seems useful to call to mind one of Otto Brusiin's central statements:

> "Wenn der praktisch tätige Jurist in seinem juristischen Denken auf die Billigkeit zurückgreift, so kann dies eine Durchbrechung der im Gesetze niedergelegten Schematisierung bedeuten. Der spontane, 'natürliche' ethisch fühlende Mensch steht hier der – ebenso menschlichen – Schematisierung feindlich gegenüber. Ja, im Namen eines höheren Menschentums kann er sich zu der Durchbrechung seiner Rechtsordnung unbedingt verpflichtet fühlen. Die Stellung der Rechtsordnung ist also eine ambivalente. Einerseits erscheint sie als eine unerläßliche Bedingung eines jeglichen friedlichen Zusammenlebens und somit jedes kulturellen Schaffens. Andererseits kann die Rechtsordnung in einem konkreten Falle als ein erdrückender, unmenschlicher Zwang erlebt werden, dem man sich nicht unterwerfen kann, ohne die Menschenwürde zu verlieren. *Ein Widerspruch liegt hier aber nicht vor,* obgleich die Sache zuweilen so dargestellt wird. Die Existenz einer Rechtsordnung ist für den in einer Gesellschaft lebenden Menschen praktisch ebenso notwendig wie die Durchbrechung dieser Ordnung in den seltenen konkreten Situationen, bei denen der Mensch ihre Auswirkung als eine grobe Verletzung seiner Würde erlebt."[1]

---

[1] Cf. *Otto Brusiin,* Über das Juristische Denken, in: idem., Der Mensch und sein Recht. Ausgewählte rechtstheoretische Schriften, Berlin 1990, pp. 194f. (emphasis added).

("When the practising lawyer, in his legal thinking, takes recourse to equity, this may imply breaking the pattern laid down in the law. Man as a spontaneous, 'natural' being with moral sentiments, in that case, becomes the enemy of – also perfectly human – pattern-making. Still more: in the name of a superior humanity, he may even feel unconditionally obliged to break his legal order. Thus, the situation of the legal order is ambivalent. On the one hand, it seems to be a necessary condition for all peaceful coexistence and, therefore, all cultural activity. On the other, the legal order may, in a particular case, be experienced as a crushing and inhuman force one cannot submit to without loosing one's dignity. *There is, however, no contradiction in this,* although sometimes the matter is presented that way. For a human being living in a society, the existence of a legal order is practically just as necessary as is the breaking of that order in those rare particular situations where the effect of that order is experienced as a rude violation of one's dignity.")

Precisely the relationship between the legal order, understood as a "necessary condition for all peaceful coexistence" *(unerläßliche Bedingung eines jeglichen friedlichen Zusammenlebens),* and the respect of human dignity is what I wish to analyze in what follows. For reasons of simplicity, and following a proposal of Brusiin,[2] I will call this relationship the "relationship between security and equity". Brusiin is right when he says that this relationship is not contradictory, and I think one can even go one step further and defend the thesis that the negation of all equity makes security impossible. If that is so, security and equity are values which not only do not contradict each other, but which are even complementary. In order to reach that conclusion, however, several prior steps have to be taken. Therefore, it is advisable:

(1) to take a closer look at the role played by the values of security and equity in the arguments brought forward to explain the formation of, and to justify, the state;

(2) to see whether and in what sense one can say that the violation of human dignity may affect the stability of state order, and, finally,

(3) to consider the possibility of a case where the negation of all principles of equity or justice can make the existence of a state order impossible.

I. Security and Equity as Necessary Conditions for the Existence of the State

In classical versions of the rational justification of the state like those of Thomas Hobbes and John Locke, as well as in contemporary ones like those of James Buchanan and Robert Nozick, obtaining a minimum of

---

[2] Cf. *Otto Brusiin,* Über die Objektivität der Rechtsprechung, in: idem (note 1), p. 129.

security – understood as the freedom from fear to be harmed in one's physical integrity or property – seems to be a necessary condition in the explanation of the formation of a state order, that is, the implementation of a legal system provided with the power to impose sanctions and capable of heteronomously enforcing certain forms of behaviour. The argument is based on the assumption that any rational being – that is, any being able to perceive its own interests – would accept that only the existence of a coercive order can guarantee a coexistence in which the good of social peace by far exceeds the bad which may be required to maintain it.

Between the reasoning of Hobbes-Buchanan and that of Locke-Nozick, there is, however, an essential difference: according to the former, security is not only a necessary, but also a sufficient condition to explain the formation of the state, and also to justify this formation; according to the latter, it is only a necessary condition, and in order to get a full justification, one has to bring in additional values such as the consent the members of a society grant to governmental measures which, for instance, may affect their property. Therefore, the so-called "Lockean proviso" and Nozick's "side-constraints" can be used to justify civil disobedience within a given system, and even its revolutionary overthrow. It was not by chance that the British colonies in America used Locke's writings to justify their independence. Here, we seem to have a good historical example of what Brusiin has called the "breaking of the legal order" *(Durchbrechung der Rechtsordnung)* for reasons of justice or equity.

In other words: In the first case, the issue is rather the *explanation* of the formation of the State which, at the same time, serves as a justifying reason; in the second case, an important difference between explanation and *justification* is introduced. In the first case, attention focuses on the *existence* of the state, in the second, the question is whether its existence is *ethically acceptable*. In the Hobbes-Buchanan version, the members of a society decide to found a coercive state order for purely prudential reasons (they prefer having their behaviour coercively restricted to the danger of arbitrarily being harmed by their fellow-men). Thus, they intend to maximise the pursuit of their interests.

But even Hobbes already knew that the line of maximisation of one's self-interest has its shortcomings with respect to what it can contribute to justification, and he could not overcome the difficulty of giving a totally satisfactory answer to why someone who wishes consistently to pursue his self-interest should not also wish to enjoy the double advantage of having others fulfil a contract while not fulfilling it himself. Such behaviour can only be qualified as parasitic if one transcends the level of self-interest and accepts other, additional values like equity or impartiality as well. Hobbes, of course, was not willing to take this step; instead, he preferred to stigmatise the question as the question of the "Foole" which did not require any answer.

One of the latest – unsuccessful – attempts to give an answer to the question of the "Foole" from the perspective of the rational pursuit of self-interest has been that of David Gauthier. But again, in the solution he proposes, it is not at all clear why in the pursuit of their interests individuals should refrain from cheating and fraud, and not fully exploit their strategic advantages.[3] Gauthier's failure shows very clearly that purely strategic arguments are insufficient for a moral foundation of state organisation. In the words of Georg Henrik von Wright[4]:

> "The possibility of adding to the blessings of the reign of justice the profits of unjust action, in short: the possibility of that which we have called parasitic action, constitutes an important sense in which justice and morality can be said to be *essentially* void of a utilitarian justification."

Therefore, Brusiin is right with the observation quoted at the beginning which states that there is no contradiction between the value of security and the value of equity: because the first one has to be analyzed on the level of *prudential* reasons, and the second on the level of *moral* reasons. However, I do think that the thesis which affirms that the existence of a state depends on the respect of moral principles, like human dignity, is too strong, and that in Brusiin's version it is even false, unless one brings in additional ideas – to which I will come back later. Thus, if the existence of the state can be explained with prudential reasons concerning security – and if one leaves aside the question of justification –, then I do not understand why it should be necessary to add the value of equity and to say that its violation will have the consequence that the members of the respective society will feel "unconditionally obliged" *(unbedingt verpflichtet)* to "break" the order of the state. On the other hand, maybe Brusiin's thesis has to be interpreted in a somewhat weaker sense, meaning that not necessarily the existence, but the *stability* of state order would be endangered. The thesis could then be restated as saying: "If you wish to maintain the stability of your state order, you must respect human dignity." In order to find out whether this weak version of Brusiin's thesis can be accepted, we should now take a look at the relevance of the value of human dignity as a factor of stability.

---

3 Cf. *Brian Barry,* Theories of Justice, Berkeley/Los Angeles 1989, p. 301. With respect to the proposal of an answer to the question of the "Foole" given by Gauthier; cf. *Ruth Zimmerling,* La pregunta del tonto y la respuesta de Gauthier, in: Doxa 6 (1989), pp. 49 - 76.

4 Cf. *Georg Henrik von Wright,* The Varieties of Goodness, London 1963, p. 215.

II. Human Dignity and Stability

In what measure can human dignity be considered to be a necessary condition for the stability of a legal order, as Brusiin seems to think? Suppose we accept the Kantian definition of human dignity as the attribute

> "eines vernünftigen Wesens, das keinem Gesetze gehorcht als dem, das es zugleich selbst gibt. ... Was einen Preis hat, an dessen Stelle kann auch etwas anderes als Äquivalent gesetzt werden; was dagegen über allen Preis erhaben ist, mithin kein Äquivalent verstattet, das hat eine Würde."[5]

> („... of a reasonable being which only obeys the law it, at the same time, gives itself. ... Whatever has a price, that can be replaced by something else as an equivalent; but whatever is above any price, and therefore does not allow for any equivalent, that has dignity.")

Let us also accept that slavery is an institution which violates human dignity. One might think, however, that even a slave could give himself the law establishing slavery, and that he could accept it, because he has read Aristotle[6] and now believes that slavery is a natural phenomenon and that the best thing for him to do is to remember the utility it can give him. As an alternative, he could agree with James S. Buchanan's reflections[7] and believe that

> "[a] contract of slavery would, as other contracts, define individual rights, and, to the extent that this assignment is mutually accepted, mutual gains may be secured from the consequent reduction in defence and predation effort".

For both of these possible explanations of the behaviour of the slave, the observation of Bernard Williams applies, that[8]

> "it is precisely a mark of extreme exploitation or degradation that those who suffer it do *not* see themselves differently from the way they are seen by the exploiters; either they do not see themselves as anything at all, or they acquiesce passively in the role for which they have been cast".

History clearly shows that it is perfectly possible to have a state based on slavery where even the slaves themselves prefer this type of social order to the alternative of dying. This in itself already shows the insufficiency of any factual consent as a criterion for the moral quality of a legal or state system. This cannot come as a surprise if one remembers

---

5 Cf. *Immanuel Kant,* Grundlegung zur Metaphysik der Sitten, Hamburg 1957, p. 58.

6 Cf. *Aristotle,* Politics, Book I, 1254b.

7 Cf. *James S. Buchanan,* The Limits of Liberty – Between Anarchy and Leviathan, Chicago/London 1975, p. 60.

8 Cf. *Bernard Williams,* The Idea of Equality, in: Peter Laslett/W. G. Runciman (eds.), Philosophy, Politics and Society, (Second Series), Oxford 1967, pp. 110 - 131, here pp. 117f.

that the argument of factual consent can be understood as a specific version of the utilitarian argument to which the considerations of Georg Henrik von Wright quoted earlier apply.

One could, however, continue this line of reasoning and claim that the stability of such an organisation would be severely threatened; in other words: that individual liberty and a minimum of equality are necessary conditions for the stability of a legal system. Following this line of argument, one could even think that the masters themselves, rather than the slaves, would want to abolish slavery because of its negative effect on the stability of the system of domination. This is the argument of Norbert Hoerster:

> "Die Sklaven müssen sich realistischerweise sagen, daß die Nicht-Sklaven, die Freien sie ausnutzen; daß diese von den moralischen und rechtlichen Institutionen deutlich mehr profitieren als sie und zwar auf ihre Kosten. Es liegt nahe, daß den Sklaven das Bewußtsein dieser Situation zu einer Quelle ständiger Unzufriedenheit wird. Aufstände und Vergeltungsmaßnahmen gegen die Unterdrücker können die Folge sein. ... Selbst in einer relativ stabilen Sklavengesellschaft müssen den Freien die Aussicht auf Aufstände und Vergeltungsmaßnahmen, die erst seinen Kindern oder Enkeln drohen mögen, vernünftigerweise mit Sorge erfüllen."[9]
>
> ("The slaves, looking at reality, must become aware of the fact that the non-slaves, the free men are exploiting them; that they profit substantially more from the existing moral and legal institutions - at the expense of the slaves. It seems plausible that being conscious of that situation will become a constant source of frustration for the slaves. Rebellions and retaliatory measures against the oppressors could be the consequence. ... Even in a relatively stable society based on slavery, the perspective of rebellions and retaliation against his children or grandchildren must trouble any free man.")

Unfortunately, the legitimacy of a legal or political system (understood as the coincidence of its norms with the principles and rules of ethics) is neither necessary nor sufficient for the system's stability. Societies based on slavery like those of Spanish America in colonial times have enjoyed remarkable stability during three centuries. When, in the 17th century, Simón Bolívar asked permission from the Spanish Crown to import 4.000 slaves, he probably did not worry too much about the security of the grandson who was to carry his name and become the Liberator of Venezuela; and when the latter ordered to free the slaves, he did this not out of fear for the stability of the reigning system, but on the contrary, precisely in order to overthrow this system with the help of black soldiers.

Brusiin's weak thesis - in the sense that respecting human dignity is a necessary condition for the stability of any state - can be understood as

[9] Cf. *Norbert Hoerster*, Moralbegründung ohne Metaphysik, in: Erkenntnis 19 (1983), pp. 225 - 238, here p. 237.

a technical rule for governments worrying about the stability of their regime. Whether or not this rule is correct depends on the circumstances in which it is applied. Under the circumstances that held in Machiavelli's Italy, the technical rules he formulated for his prince (that is, not to comply with the principles of ethics) may have been correct. In a representative democracy, Brusiin's phrase is correct *by definition* of representative democracy: for its stability, this system presupposes as a necessary condition the existence of a homogeneous society, where by "homogeneous" I understand that all members of the society are entitled to the means for satisfying their basic needs, that means, to the respect of their dignity as human beings. In both cases, the correctness of the technical rule linking the respect (or: non-respect) for human dignity to the stability of the legal or political system depends on the circumstances characterising that system.

We can, therefore, conclude that Brusiin's thesis in its weak version – that is, interpreted as a technical rule for assuring the stability of a legal-political system – is false if it is phrased as a universal proposition valid for all legal systems, but that it is correct *by definition* if it refers specifically to representative democracies.

At this juncture, someone might have difficulty to understand my initial claim that I basically agree with Brusiin's theses.

In order to show that I really do agree with him, I would like to call to mind two other observations by Brusiin:

"Diese konstante Spannung (zwischen Sicherheit und Billigkeit, E. G. V.) ist nicht nur bei der Arbeit des Richters feststellbar. Sie ist eine invariante Eigenschaft allen rechtlichen Denkens. Es sei besonders hervorgehoben, daß sie keineswegs nur ausnahmsweise erscheint, sondern daß sie – schwächer oder stärker – *immer* das rechtliche Denken begleitet. Nur wenn die Toleranzschwelle überschritten wird, kommt ein genaues Innehalten der vom Rechte aufgestellten Schemen dem Denkenden als 'unbillig' vor, und er sucht einer solchen Entscheidung auszuweichen. Wenn man die Grade der Spannung auf einer fortlaufenden Skala abbildet, bekommt man ein anschauliches Bild von der Dialektik des rechtlichen Denkens."[10]

"Das positive Recht wird auf die Gerechtigkeit in doppelter Weise bezogen. Einerseits hat der Mensch ein Bedürfnis, seine positive Rechtsordnung zu idealisieren, sie im großen und ganzen als gerecht anzusehen. Diese konservative Funktion der Gerechtigkeit ist wohl die überwiegende. Andererseits kann die Gerechtigkeit der positiven Rechtsordnung gegenübergestellt werden."[11]

("This constant tension [between security and equity, E. G. V.] can be seen not only in the work of the judge. It is an invariant property of all legal thinking. It

10 *Brusiin* (note 2).

11 Cf. *Brusiin* (note 1), p. 251.

should be especially emphasised that it by no means appears only in exceptional cases, but that it *always* – in a stronger or weaker form – accompanies legal thinking. Only when the limit of tolerance has been surpassed, exact compliance with the patterns established by the law seems 'inequitable' to the thinker, and he tries to evade such a decision. If one represents the degrees of tension on a continuous scale, one gets an illustrative picture of the dialectics of legal thinking."

"Positive law is doubly linked to justice. On the one hand, man feels the need to idealise his positive legal order and to consider it, on the whole, as just. This conservative function of justice probably is the more important one. But on the other hand, the positive legal order can also be confronted with justice.")

The need for idealisation to which Brusiin refers here can be seen in connection with the necessity that at least the officials of a system adopt what H. L. A. Hart has called the "internal point of view" towards the rules of their system. For the area of political theory, I propose to call "legitimation" the attitude of those who adopt such an internal point of view. Legitimation – or, what is the same: the internal point of view – is then a necessary, but not a sufficient condition for the existence of a legal or State order.

Here, I would like to point out a claim that is implicit in the statements of Brusiin I quoted and which I think is correct, namely that the judges and any other person agreeing with the existing legal system must think that this system satisfies the requirements of justice. In the explicit words of Otto Brusiin, these persons form part of the "active nuclear group" *(aktive Kerngruppe)* of the dominant basic social attitude. Therefore,

"[d]ie Individuen der Kerngruppe versuchen den Individuen der Gefolgschaft die 'richtige' Einstellung beizubringen und sie bei ihnen fortwährend zu stärken".[12]

("[t]he individuals of the nuclear group try to teach the individuals of the follower group the 'right' attitude and to reinforce it continuously.")

This claim of representing the 'right' attitude is what elsewhere I have called the "claim of legitimacy": the judge who pronounces a sentence has the claim that his verdict is not only legally, but also morally correct (in accordance, of course, with his own interpretation of morality). From the point of view of the "nuclear group" *(Kerngruppe)*, legitimation and legitimacy coincide. It is, therefore, not by chance that Max Weber in his treatment of the legitimation of the different forms of domination talked of *Legitimitätsglauben* (which literally means "legitimacy belief"). With the claim of legitimacy, it is just as with the claim of truth made by someone who says to believe in the truth of some descriptive proposition.

---

12 Cf. *Otto Brusiin,* Zum Ehescheidungsproblem, Hyvinkää 1959, pp. 18f.

Obviously, if one believes in the truth of *P* one considers *P* to be true. From the point of view of the person holding a belief, belief and truth coincide. In the words of Ludwig Wittgenstein[13]:

> "Gäbe es ein Verbum mit der Bedeutung 'fälschlich glauben', so hätte das keine sinnvolle erste Person im Indikativ des Präsens."
>
> ("If there were a verb meaning 'to believe wrongly', it would have no meaningful first person indicative present.")

Now, obviously, a belief – be it a belief in truth or in legitimacy – wants to be consistent. Therefore, in the case of a *Legitimitätsglaube,* that is, a claim of legitimacy, the belief goes into a crisis when there arises a conflict between the dispositions of the legal order and the moral convictions of the holder of the belief.

Arguably, this must not always be the case, and there can possibly be individual exceptions. Not to admit this would, without doubt, be rather unrealistic. In the case of the judges, Hart probably is right when he says that in their application of law they do not necessarily have to presuppose the moral legitimacy of the legislature:

> "Thus individual judges may explain or justify their acceptance of the legislator's enactments by saying that they simply wish to continue in an established practice or that they have sworn on taking office to continue it or that they had tacitly agreed to do so by accepting the office of judge. All this would be compatible with judges either having no belief at all concerning the moral legitimacy of the legislature or even with their believing that it had none."[14]

One could even admit that some legislators sometimes give their approval to a law although they are convinced that it is morally wrong. They may do this out of party loyalty, or because they are afraid of loosing their mandate, that is, for prudential reasons. In the case of judges, it is assumed that the law offers them "peremptory reasons". But the question is precisely whether this attitude may be conceptually generalised. The concept of peremptory reasons itself depends on attributing authority to someone to formulate these reasons. Thus, those who claim to be the highest authority of a system cannot refer to peremptory reasons themselves, if they do not want to get caught in an infinite regress. Instead, they have to, in the strong sense of the word, be attached to their norms, that is, they have to give them their moral approval.

Brusiin rightly underlines the "conservative function of justice *(konservative Funktion der Gerechtigkeit)*". This function can be explained as a result of the attachment to the norms one considers just. This type

---

13 Cf. *Ludwig Wittgenstein,* Philosophische Untersuchungen, in: idem, Schriften, Frankfurt am Main 1960, pp. 279 - 544, here p. 500.

14 Cf. *H. L. A. Hart,* Essays on Bentham – Jurisprudence and Political Theory, Oxford 1982, p. 265.

of attachment is referred to in what could be called a weak version of Brusiin's thesis. A strong version would, in addition, include the requirement that the norms one is attached to must also satisfy the principles of a universally valid ethics. But Brusiin does not need to adopt such a strong thesis in order to demonstrate that legal thinking always is accompanied by a certain tension between the demands of the legal norms and one's own conception of justice. In some cases, the judge, or the lawyer in general, who thinks that a solution given by the law does not satisfy the moral principles he sustains may take recourse to the idea of axiological gaps and, according to Brusiin,[15] reach an "equity sentence" *(Billigkeitsurteil)* as a "gap sentence" *(Lückenurteil)*. But once this tension surpasses the limit of tolerance, the idea of justice no longer plays a conservative role and, instead, becomes a factor of crisis. In that case, the system cannot be accepted any longer, and disobedience becomes a duty. It is interesting to note that to reinforce his thesis Brusiin makes use of a quote by someone who should be assumed to be anything but a defender of the link between law and morality, namely: Bertrand Russell. In case of severe conflict between the dispositions of a legal order and the moral convictions of the addressee of those norms, Russell says, "it would be a sin to obey".[16]

Because of the danger of "subjective arbitrariness" *(subjektive Willkür)*, in the case of an "equity sentence" *(Billigkeitsurteil)* Brusiin suggests to use "extreme caution" *(äußerste Zurückhaltung)*, especially when "the content of an equity sentence is not unequivocally supported by the dominant legal conviction" *(eine Billigkeitserwähnung inhaltlich nicht in ganz eindeutiger Weise von der herrschenden Rechtsüberzeugung gestützt wird)*.[17] With respect to this, however, although the "dominant legal conviction" certainly can function as a barrier against arbitrary subjectiveness, I think we should be very careful. Not all "dominant legal convictions" can serve as a guide, unless one believes factual consensus to be a criterion of moral rightness, thus erasing the difference between *legitimation* and *legitimacy*. The "dominant legal convictions" of Nazi judges were perfectly compatible with, and stimulated, the barbarities committed in the field of German law between 1933 and 1945. There we have an example of cases where, without any doubt, dissent would be morally much more salutary than consent.

But Brusiin is right in his call for caution if what he wants to prevent is arbitrariness. Arbitrariness obviously affects legal security, in the sense not only of the guarantee of peaceful coexistence, but also of the

15 Cf. *Brusiin* (note 2), p. 89.

16 Cf. the quote of *Bertrand Russell* in Otto Brusiin (note 2).

17 Ibid., p. 90.

"predictability of legal decisions" *(Voraussehbarkeit der rechtlichen Entscheidungen).*[18] But, in order to carry somewhat further the analysis of the question to what extent arbitrariness may imply a radical violation of all human dignity, and in what sense the values of equity and security not only are not mutually exclusive, but mutually require each other, I think it is advisable to return to the reflections of Otto Brusiin I quoted at the beginning.

III. Security and Equity as Values Mutually Requiring Each Other

I just said that the only legal and political system that guarantees full satisfaction of the values of security and equity is that of representative democracy. History offers a great variety of systems where the respect of equity (or, if you prefer, of human dignity) differed in intensity, without any noticeable effect on security (in the double sense of peaceful coexistence and predictability of legal decisions). As is well-known, for a number of authors, the so-called racial laws of Nuremberg, by clearly establishing the facts of penal offenses, contributed to increase security in the sense that, for example, they made it clearly predictable that mixed marriages between Aryans and Jews were null and void. Thus, Hans Buchheim was able to say[19]:

> "Die Nürnberger Gesetze (waren) geeignet, auf dem Gebiet der Diskriminierung der Juden die bis dahin vorherrschende, alle Arten von Terror begünstigende Rechtsunsicherheit zu beenden; sie schufen eine Norm, die den Opfern gewisse Schutzmöglichkeiten versprach. *Natürlich war der materielle Gehalt der Rassengesetze Unrecht,* im Gegensatz zu den bis dahin herrschenden Verhältnissen war es aber berechenbares Unrecht, und die Erfahrung des Lebens unter totalitärer Herrschaft lehrt, daß dies leichter zu ertragen ist, als die reine unberechenbare Willkür..."

> ("The Nuremberg laws [were] able, in the area of the discrimination of the Jews, to end the reigning legal insecurity which had fomented all kinds of terror; they created a norm that promised certain possibilities of protection to the victims. *Obviously, the material content of the racial laws was wrong [Unrecht],* but contrary to the circumstances that had been reigning until then, this wrongness was calculable, and the experience of life under totalitarian rule teaches one that this is easier to bear than pure, incalculable arbitrariness...")

Such calculable injustice *(berechenbares Unrecht)* was one form of guaranteeing legal security, understood as the predictability of judicial decisions, and it corresponded with the internal point of view of those in power and of a considerable portion of the population of Nazi Germany. It

---

18 Ibid., p. 89.

19 Cf. *Hans Buchheim,* Die Struktur der nationalsozialistischen Herrschaft, in: idem, Anatomie des SS-Staates, Vol. 1, 3rd ed., Munich, pp. 20f.

also was a form of legitimation sustained by the dominant legal opinion. That this legitimation had nothing to do with the legitimacy – or rather illegitimacy – of the system, in the sense I have proposed, is obvious and again shows the convenience of a conceptual distinction between legitimation and legitimacy. Therefore, in the case of totalitarian systems, there is not necessarily any conflict between security and injustice.

Now, Brusiin poses the question whether there is some legal-political system in which the violation of all justice also implies the impossibility of security, in the double sense of the word. Such a system would have to employ a formally and substantially arbitrary procedure for the application of sanctions, erase all differences between the legally guilty and the innocent, and even show a certain tendency to punish precisely those persons who – even according to the dispositions of the system itself – are innocent.

The Nazi regime included totally innocent persons in the category of the guilty, since it imposed "punishment" on persons who had not committed any action or omission; only for racial or religious reasons they were considered addressees of state sanctions. The corresponding dispositions, which without doubt must be qualified as an expression of barbarism, nevertheless permitted identification of the "guilty" and, in that sense, did guarantee a certain degree of legal security.

The decisive step towards the elimination of all traces of legal security takes place when the class of the guilty is open, that is, when the regime does not offer any criterion of delimitation. In this context, it is interesting to look at Art. 22 of the *Principles of Criminal Jurisdiction of the Soviet Union* of 1937 which said:

> "Punishment in the form of exile can be applied by a sentence of the State Prosecutor against persons recognised as being socially dangerous, without any criminal proceedings being taken against these persons on charges of committing a specific crime or of a specific offense and, also, even in those cases where these persons are acquitted by a court of the accusation of committing a specific crime."[20]

In my own country, between 1976 and 1983, a similar system was established that can certainly be called a system of state terrorism. My proposal for a definition of such *state terrorism* is the following:

> State terrorism is a form of exercising state power whose rule of recognition, aimed at provoking generalised fear,

[20] Cf. *A. James Gregor*, Fascism's Philosophy of Violence and the Concept of Terror, in: David C. Rapoport/Yonah Alexander (eds.), The Morality of Terrorism – Religious and Secular Justifications, New York 1989, p. 161.

- permits and/or commands the secret, unpredictable and diffuse application – even to clearly innocent people – of coercive measures prohibited by the proclaimed legal order,
- obstructs or nullifies judicial activity, and
- transforms the government into an active contender in the struggle for power.[21]

A legal-political system of this type must be clearly distinguished from Nazi totalitarianism and from fundamentalist totalitarianism. While in the latter cases, the class of the "good" and the "bad" is delimited by clear criteria of inclusion and exclusion, and it is, therefore, relatively easy to determine who belongs to which class, in the case of state terrorism one cannot exclude the possibility that those who defend or support state terrorism end up as their own victims, precisely because the measures are diffuse and unpredictable.

In the recent history of Argentina, which is full of all kinds of atrocities, such cases have happened. The fanatic of state terrorism, if he wants to be consistent, cannot *a posteriori* feel surprised about his own personal tragedy; he must be willing to accept that he and his family may be sacrificed arbitrarily, and he even must be prepared to sustain that this arbitrariness is just. Paradoxically, the consistency of the fanatic thus leads to an attitude which is close to insanity: whoever practices terrorism (whether state terrorism or another) must uphold, by definition, that he is morally justified – in the name of ideals he is attached to by an act of faith – to destroy innocent lives; personally, he qualifies himself as innocent, and he also includes into this class the persons he most cares about and wishes to defend against the "enemy"; but, because of his terrorist beliefs, he must admit that an effective and justifiable form of such defense is to concede the possibility of his own destruction or that of the persons dearest to him, precisely because they are "innocent".

The means characteristic of state terrorism imply a rule of recognition that contradicts the central point not only of any possible *justification* of the state, but also of any *explanation* of its genesis. It does, in fact, not only violate the Lockean "proviso" or Nozick's "side constraints" – not to mention the ethical criterion of impartiality or the respect of human dignity as defended by Brusiin. It also brings back the conditions of the pre-state situation, and in a stronger form still than the one imagined by Hobbes: While in the Hobbesian state of nature the wolf-men all had approximately the same strength, in the case of state terrorism the gov-

21 Cf. *Ernesto Garzón Valdés,* El terrorismo de Estado. El problema de su legitimación e ilegitimidad, in: Diánoia 1991, pp. 89 - 117, here p. 101.

ernment itself is a "howling wolf". This expression is not merely a literary metaphor: it was used as a justificatory argument by one of the lawyers of the Argentinean military junta who said that "when living among wolves, one must howl like them".[22] In such a situation, the extreme violation of equity makes security impossible, which means that the values of equity and security interlace in such a way as to threaten the very existence of the state. It is no accident that the existence of state-terrorist regimes is always declared as being transitional, as a necessary step towards another, allegedly definite form of state (as in the Argentinean case), or as a means to overcome a "crisis" of the system (as in the Soviet case).

Otto Brusiin has indicated repeatedly that in his theory of law there are three fundamental concepts: basic attitude, legal norm, and behaviour *(Grundeinstellung, Rechtsnorm und Verhalten)*. If one applies these concepts to the legal-political system of state terrorism, one can easily infer that the basic attitude *(Grundeinstellung)* of those who adopt an internal point of view with respect to its rule of recognition is the attitude of suicidal fanaticism. The *legal norms* no longer fulfil their technical function of guiding the *behaviour* of judges and citizens: according to James Gregor,[23] the typical question of the victims of Soviet terrorism was "Why?". The same was true in Argentina under the still not very remote military dictatorship; only that in Argentina, the apologists of the regime had an answer which, although void of any content, stimulated the imagination of those who gave that answer by offering them the possibility to give it the content they wished. The answer was: *por algo será* – "there must be some reason". In the field of political or ethical justification, this answer thus played the same role as in scientific investigation the well-known formula "Every event has its cause" – a statement lacking all possibility of falsification.

In such a situation, one easily understands that the violation of the corresponding regime's legal dispositions may be considered an act of self-defense, and that everybody, as a potential victim of the regime, may feel authorised to exercise it. The systematic elimination of all criteria for the identification of the guilty and the innocent constitutes, in any society, the extreme of all possible violations of equity, and the most serious insult against human dignity, no matter how weak a conception of the content of this dignity one has.

---

22 Ibid., p. 105.

23 Cf. *A. James Gregor* (note 20), pp. 161f.

IV. Conclusion

After the reflections so far presented, the question remains, finally, what we can infer for the relationship between security and equity from the statement of Otto Brusiin which I initially declared to agree with, and from the other quotes I have used in order to present his thinking. In my opinion, one can say, at least, the following:

(i) Extreme arbitrariness, that is, the constant and indiscriminate violation of human dignity by the government, throws society back into a pre-state situation. This shows

(ii) that there is a relevant relationship between security and equity which, in extreme cases, affects the very existence of legal and state order;

(iii) that state terrorism can be considered the prime example of the necessary reciprocal conditioning of security and equity;

(iv) that legal norms are not merely a means to regulate social behaviour, but also always include a claim of correctness or justice; and

(v) that, therefore, a complete analysis of any positive legal order must also include the study of its claims of moral correctness.

To reach this conclusion, one does not need to take recourse to the arguments of legal naturalism, or to the belief in a social order that allegedly should be guided by what is believed to be divine commands. Instead, it is enough to start from "methodological atheism" *(methodologischer Atheismus)*[24] like that proposed by Brusiin, which takes into account the "dialectics of legal thinking" *(Dialektik des rechtlichen Denkens)*.

To what extent it may be possible, starting from Otto Brusiin's anthropological concern and from his interest in the historical development of social structures, to establish a conception of human dignity that satisfies the ethical requirements of impartiality or universalisability – that is a topic which must be left to another Brusiin Lecture.

[24] Cf. *Brusiin*, Über das juristische Denken (note 1), p. 262.

RECHTSTHEORIE 28 (1997), S. 219 - 234
Duncker & Humblot, 12165 Berlin

LAW AS INSTITUTIONAL NORMATIVE ORDER

By Neil MacCormick, Edinburgh

Otto Brusiin was of the same generation as my own parents, and continued actively contributing to legal theory and comparative law on the international stage until 1973. Although he was at his most active during the years in which I was embarking on my apprenticeship as a scholar in legal theory, I never had the good fortune to meet him. I have become acquainted with his ideas through Professor Urpo Kangas' excellent edition of his selected jurisprudential works in German, prefaced by Kangas' concise but sympathetic intellectual biography and analytical-critical account of Brusiin's main ideas. Perhaps, though, what I should really say is that Kangas' work has been my only direct source of contact with Brusiin. It is impossible to overlook the extent to which he influenced a generation or two of Finnish scholars, including such figures as Aulis Aarnio, Kaarlo Tuori, Jyrki Uusitalo, Hannu Tapani Klami, Lars D. Eriksson, Eerik Lagerspetz, Juha Pöyhönen, Urpo Kangas himself and quite a few others from whom I have over the years learned many things. My indirect debt to Brusiin is therefore a very large one, and I hope I shall succeed in repaying it in this lecture.

Finland is a small Northern country of great cultural and intellectual vitality whose special contribution to the world has persisted despite the fact that for many centuries Finland was to a greater or lesser extent politically absorbed into larger totalities, sometimes to the West, sometimes to the East. The years of Otto Brusiin's active life were those in which modern Finland achieved her full standing as an independent state with reasonably cordial relations to both of the great power blocks of the cold war world, holding somehow a position of equilibrium between them, and avoiding over-dependence on either. There was a time when the term "Finlandisation" was used in a somewhat sneering way, if not even as an actual term of abuse. Yet to many of us it seemed that the impossible balancing act, which the Finns had shown to be possible after all, was one of the few signs of real hope in very difficult times. My first visit to Finland for a three-day seminar in Espoo in 1979 with a day's visit for further seminar sessions in Turku was an extraordinarily exciting experience. That first acquaintance has been followed over the years, through quite regular visits, and through frequent intellectual contacts with Finnish colleagues in other places, by a sense of deepening respect for Finland as a country and for the special contribution Finnish scholars have been making to the contemporary international ferment of interest in philosophical aspects of legal scholarship.

Scotland is also a small northern country, and also has, I hope, a certain intellectual and cultural vitality and distinctiveness despite political absorption for nearly three hundred years in a larger United Kingdom. I value especially my contacts and friendships here in Finland and in the other Nordic countries on account of the similarities as well as differences of our political and cultural situations, as well as, of course, the many historical connections we have enjoyed. In paying tribute to the role Otto Brusiin played in building a distinctive and self-confident legal theoretical community among Finnish scholars, I must not overlook another powerful and benevolent influence, that of Georg Henrik von Wright who expresses in his ancestral connections the many links that have existed between Scotland and the Baltic countries, as well as having contributed to Finnish philosophy a distinctive logical-analytical style, of course with important links to Wittgenstein's Cambridge and Wittgenstein's Vienna; but also exhibiting independent genius in the application of logic in the normative realm.

We Europeans live now in the twilight of the sovereign state as that emerged from older institutions of feudal monarchies and empires, exploding into life with the fall of the Bastille, not to mention, a little later, Napoleon's "whiff of grapeshot". The collapse of the experiment of one-party communist socialism coincided with the ending of the first three decades of the European Economic Community, now, with its sister communities, subsumed within the European Union so confidently announced in the Treaty of Maastricht. As we prepare for the enlargement of the Union, we are more and more aware of living within legal frameworks that go "beyond the sovereign state". For us in Scotland as for you in Finland, there is inevitable concern over the question how hospitable this new order will be to the continuing vitality of small and peripheral polities such as ours. Many of us will envy you Finns the fact that, albeit full state sovereignty is a thing of the past, you will at least have the full standing of member state in the Community and Union.

In any event, I think that the elision of states as all-sufficient sovereign entities will provide a better framework for mutual and equal respect of cultures and regional variances than what has gone before. And we who are on the northern and western peripheries of this great Europe that emerges will need to maintain an ever more intense mutual regard and awareness if we are to avoid the ill-effects of any tendency to excessively centripetal forces within Europe. In that spirit, I approach the task of giving the Otto Brusiin lecture with both humility and pride. I pay homage to the memory of a fine scholar and thinker, and at the same time express my strong sense of solidarity with and indebtedness to the thriving modern Finnish jurisprudential community whose existence is, I venture to say, Brusiin's own finest memorial.

With Brusiin, I share a number of preoccupations; many common questions, but sometimes different answers. Brusiin's work expresses a sense of the locatedness of law in human communities, and its orientation to human values. Human beings, not the state, make the law. At the same time law is located at the heart of political reality, the reality of law is a political reality, and law is both dependent on and interpenetrated by political power. The ultimate legal reality is a reality of norms in human societies, the question being what distinguishes specifically legal norms from other social norms that lack the special characteristic of being norms of law. Brusiin has some penetrating things to say about this. An extended quotation here seems justified:

> Among the norms of human societies, a dichotomy can be proposed. The greater part of these norms stand in no immediate connection with organised society, that is, they are not formulated by officials ("organs"), and officials do not deal with any occurring breaches of them. Another set of norms does, however, link up with the organisation of society in so far as officials take action in respect of breaches of these norms. Officials can also formulate norms of this kind, and can confer authoritative recognition upon them. It can also be said that organised society stands behind these norms. To such norms we give the name "legal norms". Together, they constitute a complex of norms that we call "legal order".[1]

This seems to me to be both true and profound. While I may partially disagree with Brusiin about some aspects of the relationships and distinctions between the legal and the moral or the legal and the political, what I call "institutional normative order" matches very closely with these remarks of Brusiin's about the distinction between norms of the law and other social norms. I hope to make this clear in what follows. First, I discuss the differentiation of the legal from the political and the moral by introducing the idea that law should be handled as a special form of normative order, namely institutional normative order. The second part then gives an account of what is meant here by "normative order", and the third discusses the institutionalisation of normative order, concluding with observations on the characteristics of the *Rechtsstaat,* or "law-state". The conclusion of the lecture pulls all this together.

---

1 *O. Brusiin,* Der Mensch und sein Recht. Ausgewählte rechtstheoretische Schriften, Berlin 1990, pp. 143 - 144 (my translation).

I. Law and Politics, Law and Morality

The first task is to sharpen our sense of the distinction between law and the two other realms of thought and action with which it is most intimately interrelated, and yet interrelated as something conceptually distinct, a genuine third term, not simply an amalgam of the first two. Politics is concerned with law – law making and law reform, appointments to key legal offices, maintenance of the forces of law and order, supporting the rulings of the courts. Yet politics is not law, nor law politics, despite occasional assertions to the contrary from the ramparts of Critical Legal Studies. Morality is concerned with law, with the criticism of legal decisions and legal rules, with the issue of obligation to law, with question of law's claim to be genuinely normative, genuinely engaged with the world of the "ought". Yet morality is not law, nor is law morality, nor a sub-department of morality, for all that this has sometimes been claimed by thinkers in the tradition of "natural law". I want to re-apply here ideas developed in some recent papers concerning these distinctions. The key ideas are those of power, which seems to me especially focal for politics, and autonomy, which seems to me definitive for morality. Let us see how these ideas help with the distinctions sought.

Politics is a matter of power, of the actual exercise of power within human societies or communities, and of elaborating principles for the proper exercise of power. Political power is the power to direct social agencies and individuals to certain defined ends presumptively for the common good, to dispose of available goods (economic and non-economic) among persons and groups, and to protect the group against interference from agencies external to it. The power that we have in mind here is power-in-fact, not simply normative power, that is, power to make sure that somebody in fact acts in a certain way, rather than power to bring it about that somebody ought to act in a certain way. Political power is power-in-fact; but what is sometimes termed "legal power" is power of the other sort, normative power, power confined to the realm of the "ought".

Law interacts with politics in many ways; sometimes as an object over and through which political power is exercised; sometimes as a control upon the use and abuse of power. But law is not itself constituted by the power-in-fact to effect social change. Law is a form of normative order, setting patterns of right and wrong conduct and conferring powers which are normative rather than coercive in their intrinsic character. Nobody doubts that the United States Constitution conferred and still confers the normative power to ban the manufacture, sale, and consumption of alcohol for beverage purposes. If exercised, this entails that according to law alcohol ought not to be manufactured, sold, or consumed for those purposes. The experiment of the nineteen twenties, however, proved that this legal normative power was not conjoined with sufficient power-in-fact to change the drinking tastes of Americans. I hope that sufficiently exemplifies the distinction I have here in mind – politics about power, law about normative order.

Morality also concerns normative order. Morality in its most fundamental sense has to be grasped in terms akin to those of Kant or of Habermas. Morality is autonomous and universal; it is discursive and controversial. Moral principles are those we can argue out in conditions of free and uncoercive discourse, accepting that they must be universal in application and must take account of the interests and ideals of all persons capable of participating in the discourse or capable of being affected by its outcome. Each person is as competent a participant in moral discourse as every other, and the ultimate judgment of right and wrong in moral matters is for each agent a matter for decision after engagement in actual or imagined discourse with others.

Morality in a less fundamental sense is located in the common or conventional principles and rules held by persons in communities, often in connection with religious observances and traditions. To show why this sense is less fundamental, one need only ponder the question why these principles and rules have authority over an individual. One or other of only two answers is possible. Either their authority derives from the individual's willing commitment to them, or it derives from the power, however crude or subtle, of community opinion and persuasion or disapproval that keeps the individual in line. In the former case, they are incorporated in the individual's morality through autonomous choice, hence conventional morality is subordinated to individual autonomy. In the latter case, individuals are subjected to the exercise of power, however diffuse and ill-defined, and the rules of conventional morality are an element in the politics of community. If we are to understand morality as a distinct realm of thought and judgement, it can only be through giving conceptual primacy to the discursive-autonomous conception of morality.

Law resembles morality in that it is normative; it resembles conventional morality in being a normative order commonly observed in some community or society, and backed by strong pressures of opinion, and by the regularly confirmed belief that others apply norms that are regarded as common standards for the group in question. States being territorial political communities organised under governments capable of wielding coercive power over individuals and groups and in response to external forces, the law of states is backed not only by opinion but also by coercive power. But law itself is not coextensive with states, and provides criteria for rightful use of power, not being the mere creature of brute power however permanent or temporary. So law is a kind of partly actual, partly ideal, normative order observed in some ordered community or society.

Above all, law has positivity. We look to law for answers to questions about what is obligatory or not, permissible or not within some sphere of decision-making. Law lays down what *is* obligatory or permissible, not what from some ideal point of view ought to be obligatory or permissible. This is because law institutionalises decision-making. A properly taken decision that a certain rule shall be enacted into law does confer on that rule the character of being an actual rule of law. A properly taken decision about some disputed point of right between two persons settles conclusively the rights of each upon that point, just as a properly taken decision upon an accusation of crime settles conclusively the legal guilt or innocence of the accused person. Here, I share exactly in Brusiin's view.

Persons or agencies that can take such decisions – "Organs" in the terminology of Brusiin, Kelsen, and many others – decide with authority. They have legal authority to decide, and within the scope of that authority their decisions are conclusive except in so far as subject or review or appeal before agencies (organs) endowed with yet higher authority, and any such hierarchy of authority has some apex beyond which no further appeal or application for review is competent. Law thus has an authoritative character. Its authoritative character is tied up with the existence of institutionalised decision making, hence with law's institutional character. As a consequence, law can be contrasted with our fundamental conception of morality – law is heteronomous, where morality is autonomous. Morality is what an agent freely wills in a context of ideal or actual discourse; law is what is authoritatively decided in an institutional context, and has binding force as law whether or not any particular person autonomously endorses it or rejects it or subjects it to reservations of a more or less extensive kind. Whereas morality is controversial, discursive, and autonomous, law is institutional, authoritative, and heteronomous.

One manifestation of this lies in the way in which, on questions of law, there frequently seems to be a fact of the matter, checkable by reference to publicly accessible sources. If a person wants to find out whether there is a maximum speed limit on the roads of a country, or a maximum permitted level of blood alcohol for drivers, there are sources to which one can quite easily look for an answer. Explicit rules on such matters are to be found in pieces of legislation, frequently supplemented by pieces of subordinate legislation; and secondary sources such as legal text-books or government publications about road traffic assist in identifying them. On the moral question how fast it is right to drive, or how much if any alcohol it is morally acceptable to drink before driving, there is no interpersonally checkable source establishing a quantitative limit; such questions are settleable only through moral discourse, weighing relevant arguments, and establishing considerations relevant to the issue in hand. Their settlement from time to time depends on the conscientious judgement of a moral agent, whether or not in conformity with the conscientious judgement of other agents actually or potentially participating in the relevant discourse.

Conversely, the settled, positive, character of law is jurisdiction-relative. How fast one may drive is a question differently answered in different places governed by different legal systems under the jurisdiction of different organs or agencies. The fact of the legal matter is a fact about some discrete legal system, and, where the law in question is state-law, the answer normally holds good only in respect of the territory of the given state. Sixty miles per hour is the maximum permitted speed on roads in the United Kingdom other than designated Motorways, on which the maximum is seventy miles per hour. That holds good, of course, only for roads in the United Kingdom regulated by the Road Traffic Acts. If I visit another country, such as Finland, I expect the rules to be different, and even expressed in different units of measurement. Here, I have to check on maxima in terms of kilometres per hour; and so on. In each jurisdiction, I look for some distinct piece of legislation (or other authoritative law-text) that settles the matter within that jurisdiction.

Moral judgments, however personal and controversial, are not in this way relativistic. If I hold that driving above a certain speed is inherently dangerous to life and limb, or wasteful of natural resources, and if I hold that humans ought not to endanger each others' bodily safety, or make excessive demands on non-renewable resources, then I must hold that speeding is wrong wherever it may cause danger or use too much petrol. These judgments apply universally. No doubt they are susceptible only to being supported with arguments in a moral discourse, without any interpersonally authoritative source to check against; but in their own character they are universalisable claims, not restricted by jurisdiction or territoriality. Certainly, circumstances alter cases morally; but they do so in a universalisable way. The truth of moral matters is not checkable by reference to established, public and institutional sources. But their truth is an unrestricted and universal truth to the extent we can establish it at all.

The dual contrast of law with politics and with morality is crucial for the theme of today. Law is both a normative and an institutional order, and this connects it with the two poles of the contrast. As a normative order, it replicates certain features of morality, and connects necessarily to morality in certain ways. As an institutional order, it connects necessarily to politics and is in part constitutive of the political. The inquiry will proceed to deal with these two points in that order.

II. Law as Normative Order

Normative order is a kind of ideal order. At any given time we may form a view of the world as it is, including the set of ongoing human actions and intentions for action; we may set against that a view of the world as it could be or could become, leaving out certain of the actions, leaving some actual intentions abandoned or unfulfilled, while other actions take place instead of those left out, and other intentions are fostered and brought to fulfilment. A view of the world as it could be or could become is an ideal view of it. An ideal view may be constructed so as to exclude certain ways of acting on all occasions on which such action might otherwise by contemplated, and to include certain other ways of acting as always called for despite any contrary temptation.

There is a notorious ambiguity in the term "ideal" and most of its cognates in the various European languages. Sometimes we mean by it that which exists merely in idea, that is, within ideas held by some person or persons, whether for good or ill or in a neutral way. Sometimes, however, "ideal" conveys the notion of a favoured or even highly favoured idea. Normative order, of course, is ideal in the sense of the favoured or preferred idea, not merely the neutral idea. Yet it falls short of any "best of all possible worlds" perfectionism. Normative order is practical, both in the sense that it guides praxis, guides what we do, and also therefore practical in the sense of practicable. It is an order that is envisaged as a practically realisable state of the world given things as they are and persons as they are here and now; to the extent that it is realised, the world is a better, more satisfactory, world than if no such guideline were envisaged or followed. "Norms" are propositions that we formulate with reference to, and as singled-out elements of, normative order. In primary form, they are either exclusionary provisions (negative duties, prohibitions) that exclude certain ways of acting on all occasions on which such action might otherwise be contemplated, or provisions of the converse type (positive duties, obligations) that call for certain ways of acting as required of a person despite any contrary temptation, or countervailing reason for action.

This is not an attempt to explain norms or values in terms of value-free facts, of course. The notion of the "better" or "more satisfactory" built into the account of normative order as ideal order shows normative order to belong within, not independently of, values as fundamental elements in all human consciousness. Here again, I am working on the same ground as Otto Brusiin.

Also essential to making sense of these concepts is the way in which the practical concerns that which engages a person's will. Merely to envisage a possible world extrapolated from the actual one, even to think of it in some purely contemplative way as better than the actual is not to cross over into the realm of the normative. A steady commitment of the will to realisation of some ideal order as a coherent and realisable state of the world is what is required for that transition. The will directed towards realising a practicable, rationally coherent and humanly satisfactory ideal order constitutes it as normative order. Only by reference to such an order is it possible to establish the difference of right and wrong in action. Those actions are right that are not excluded from the conceived order, those that it excludes as actions and to which it denies fulfilment in intention are wrong. The dichotomy between wrong and not-wrong (or between wrong and right-in-the-sense-of-not-wrong) is the fundamental differentiation of actions or of intended or planned acts in a normative order. What a person engages upon when aiming to make normative order actual is the task of, or commitment to, avoiding wrongdoing.

The world as already-in-part-ideal order is that upon which we base our conceptions of normative order, the ideal order that would exist were practically removable imperfections purged from the way things go on now. Most promises that are made are in due course kept. Truthfulness and honesty are more frequent for most of us than lying and cheating. To formulate the principles that promises ought to be kept, that lies ought not to be told nor frauds perpetrated, is to set terms for an ideal order, but not one that stands absolutely apart from actuality, neither in terms of what is commonly done, nor in terms of what are commonly asserted as principles for ideal order by others in our communities.

Thus normative order does not stand in absolute contrast with actuality. Quite a lot of what goes on is perfectly compatible with what is right from the point of view of any reasonable moral attitude. Moreover, this is the case, at least in part, because people share legal systems and moral attitudes or converge in the moral demands and conceptions of moral order they endorse. The world as it is does not unfold independently of human wills. On the contrary, the human world-as-it-is goes on as it goes on through human choices and decisions. However imperfectly, these choices and decisions reflect and conform to the conceptions of legal and moral rectitude held by the choosing and deciding agents. So normative order as ideal order does not stand in any absolute contrast with the world as it is. Indeed, our normative commitments come out of our response to the world as it is, our satisfaction or dissatisfaction with it as it is and as it goes on, and our sense of the practicable alternatives to what does or might happen.

There are, it seems to me, three ways in which human beings come to an awareness and understanding of normative order. Through nurture, socialisation and education, we are exposed to and socialised into some common views of the right and the wrong, and gradually led to an ability to be at least partly self-regulating against the standing norms implicit, and partly explicit, in this common view. Then, in modern conditions, we fall into a series of rather institutionalised settings in which rules are made even more explicit than in the general familial and social milieu. For everyone nowadays this includes the experience of school, with compulsory attendance; for many, still, even in a secularising society, participation to some extent in a church or other structured religious observance plays an important part. Nearly everybody participates in sports and games actively or as spectator or as both, and expertise about rules of play and rules of national and international competitions organised by officials and representative bodies is at least as widespread as knowledge and understanding of state-law. Thirdly, though, state agencies such as police and courts and in a more remote way other official organs up to and including parliaments and international agencies define one particularly authoritative, explicit and highly regulated normative order for us.

At the very least, our picture of normative order emerges out of heteronomous orders, where others communicate norms to us and we learn to follow them, usually under some external incentive. Yet the learning experience is one geared to developing an at least partial autonomy. For what we learn is to monitor and guide our own conduct against criteria of right and wrong that are conventional norms in some cases and formally enacted rules in others.

In a fundamental way, though, the possibility of developing fully autonomous judgement at the end of one's learning experience is that which makes intelligible the very concept of normative order. The telos of moral development is the fully responsible moral agent who takes responsibility for his or her judgements at all levels, and whose volitional commitment to some ideal of order is categorical, not conditional. Only a being that can act in a self-regulating way, judging between possible courses of action through voluntary commitment to some rationally willed order, and seeking to realise the willed order in action, can fully grasp the concept of "wrong" action, or therefore the concept of right-as-not-wrong action. Only such a being can make full sense of auxiliary verbs such as "ought" or "should". As Thomas Reid observed in controversy with David Hume, these are terms that every moral agent understands, but that are not definable in any terms simpler than themselves.

This repeats but generalises the thesis that autonomy is fundamental to morality. Conceptually, it is fundamental to any idea of normative order. For in the last result only an autonomous being can respond through acts of volition to the requirements of normative order. Normative order guides choices, but does not cause them. Choices are voluntary responses to an idea of order, not conditioned reflexes. On the other hand, the concept of a rationally coherent order in which universalisable principles find their place presupposes the agent's exposure to some conventional or institutional social ordering initially heteronomous in character from the agent's point of view. In the development of moral agency, heteronomy precedes autonomy.

III. Law as Institutional

Necessarily, normative order involves judgement. Norms are fragments drawn from a presupposed ideal order in the sense indicated. They are exclusionary or mandatory prescriptions that posit some course of conduct as wrong, or as obligatory. To engage with a norm as an acting subject is to judge what must be done in a given context; to reflect in normative terms upon one's own or another's conduct in a given setting is to judge, against some envisaged norm, whether what was done ought to have been done or ought not to have been done. The judgement that an act ought not to have been done normally entails a consequential judgement of the measure of penitence or restitution, or of censure, that is apt to the case. All in all, to think normatively is to think judgementally. This is a general and significant truth about all forms of normative order.

Judgement is sometimes purely personal and autonomous; sometimes it is conventional and heteronomous, without being institutionalised. It can also, however, be institutionalised, or, if you will, organized. A third party can be a relatively impartial judge between two persons on whom some norm impinges differentially. Over some range of topics, some persons may acquire a standing role as judges, to whom reference may be made; it can come about that the judgement of such persons comes to be mandatory within some normative order, in the sense that a person who wishes action taken in virtue of some normative judgement must either handle the matter in a purely voluntary way, or resort to compulsory action only under judgement of such a judge. Then appeals may or may not be allowed; but once judgement is institutionalised, there has to be some rule about the finality of judgment; a rule that it is obligatory to accept and carry out the judgement of the ultimate court, and that it is forbidden to take any further action beyond that ultimately authorised under the final judgement.

Norms involve judgement, and judgement, as we noted, is either personal and autonomous or in some measure institutionalised. Institutionalisation of judgement is a fundamental feature of the organization of normative orders. In one form or another, it occurs in a wide variety of settings, through churches, sporting organisations, commercial guilds and leagues, international organizations and agencies; and also, of course, paradigmatically in the state.

An inevitable effect of institutionalisation of judgement, especially where there comes into being a group or a corps of judges acting in a coordinated way under a common structure of appeals, is that normative order must come to be conceived as systemic in character; and the system in question necessarily possesses, as Teubner and Luhmann point out, a self-referential quality. For it has to be a question in any dispute what the governing norm is and how it is to be interpreted. Finality of judgement entails final authority on the question what counts as a binding norm, and how it bears on the case. What makes the judgement final is a norm of the normative order that makes respect for judgements obligatory in every case; but the judgement that such a norm, or any other norm, belongs to the order, is itself one which can only be pronounced with final effect by an appropriate judge or court. And the same postulated normative order is that which makes a given judge or court appropriate, or (in the more technical term) "competent" to judge on the question.

Whenever this is so, it follows that, relative to any institutional normative system, there is a way, *conclusive within the system* for determining what counts as an authoritative norm of the system, or a definitely established right or duty of some person under the system. There is even a way of determining what counts as a person under the system, and what kinds of practical social and business arrangements can be set up with binding effect in the system. The way is, of course, that of recourse to the judgement of those competent to judge. As Brusiin also remarks, although questions about sales or marriages matter to us in quite diverse ways in the ordinary social milieu, what counts in law as a "sale" or a "marriage" is a question which the law-courts necessarily have ultimate authority to determine. And they have associated authority to say what ulterior legal rights, duties, powers and the like follow consequentially upon the existence of a sale or a marriage according to law. But which law-courts? Could there be merchants' tribunals deciding about sales? Or sporting tribunals deciding about the valid transfer through "sale" of a footballer's contract? Or Church Courts deciding about marriages?

As we know, each of these is possible. There can be tribunals of many kinds, and these can deal with similar questions affecting the same human individuals. But the characteristic of an institutional normative order is that competent judgement in it is conclusive within its own order, except to the extent that there is coordinated cross-recognition of different orders, as obtained between Pope and Emperor in the middle ages, or between European Communities and member-state legal orders today. Where a plurality of judgements each conclusive within a particular order can be passed, the question is: Which ought to prevail? As a question within a self-referential system, such a question is of course self-answering. As a question for a person confronted by competing judgements of substantially the same question in practically different senses, the issue is which to respect, on grounds external to the self-referential answer provided by rival normative orders? Shall a state-court decree of divorce, or a church-court prohibition or nullification of it be taken as final? Shall the judgement of the state tribunal or the Trade Union tribunal be observed? And so on.

The answer to the question "Which to respect?" has both prudential and moral aspects. Which ought one to respect all things considered? Which is it least disadvantageous, all things considered to ignore? In case of conflict the answer to the latter question, the prudential answer, will be considerably affected both by the weight and balance of conventional opinions and by power-relations, and these will also be relevant, though less weightily, to the former, the moral question. But in so far as power-relations enter the question, the issue is, according to the earlier analysis, one of politics. Whoever can make a judgement prevail in the last resort, in the sense of its being carried through by main force if necessary, and can reliably and predictably enforce such judgements in the general run, has political power; and that political power backs and to a degree reinforces the authority and prestige of the tribunal whose judgement is enforced and that of the normative order to which the tribunal self-referentially belongs.

In the World as it has been, and still to a very large extent is, power of the relevant kind has been territorially concentrated, and each relevant territory has been that of a state. The coercively predominant normative orders have been those of states, though they have rarely if ever succeeded in absolutely eliminating rival orders of one kind or another. This is why there has been such a tendency to take for granted the equation of "law" with "state-law", though this has had serious distorting effects for legal theory.

Two obviously significant aspects of the interrelation of coercive power with normative order (thus also the interrelation of state with law) are of course that of executive power and that of legislative power. The executive possesses the direct command of the agencies of organised physical coercion that can back up the power of judgement – or, in cases of serious breakdown, disown and overthrow it. The legislature possesses, normally, the kind of democratic or quasi-democratic (or other ideological) legitimation that contributes significantly to the acceptability and durability over time of the coercive power that is organized under the executive. A delicate and shifting balance of power-relations normally obtains here. But always there is a question whether the due exercise of either legislative or executive power is a matter subjected to judicial judgement, and hence itself incorporated into the normative order which it so crucially supports. Where it is so incorporated, the state is a *Rechtsstaat,* a state-under-law, a "law-state", as Åke Frändberg tells us to call it.

In a law-state, the question what exercises of executive power are valid is a question of law; the political power of the executive is restrained under the authority of law. Likewise, it is for the courts to say what resolutions of the legislature constitute validly enacted norms of law, and how they are to be interpreted. The authority of the legislature is not a matter of democratic or ideological or hereditary legitimacy extraneous to law, but is itself conferred by law. Self-referentiality shades over into "autopoiesis". In such a state there can also be an independent profession of legal science, analysing the valid law, discussing the limits of its validity, offering interpretations that display some overall coherence and systematicity in the legal (normative) order conceived as an ideal unity. This scientific construction of order and system is itself an act of rational reconstruction extrapolating from the given material. But in turn it is a reconstruction that reinforces the conception of law as a "system", and which posits the systematicity of law as a guiding ideal for judges in particular, and also to a degree for legislators and officials of executive government.

Law conceived as institutional normative order can thus come to be constitutive of a law-state. However, as Kelsen pointed out, there are two possible ways to conceive and represent the order as a working system. The first is a dynamic way. Here, the process of change through time is central, including the way in which legal provisions themselves set the terms for valid change. This produces a representation of the order with a special focus on the processes of creation of law, and on the processes of establishing institutional arrangements (contracts, trusts, and the like) within private and lower-level public law.

When we represent a normative order in this dynamic way, we represent it in terms of the norms that regulate change, individuated as norms of competence, power-conferring rules, institutive rules of legal institutions.

The second is what Kelsen called a "static" representation. Here, we represent the order by individuating rules or norms prescribing duties, or conferring rights either permissive or beneficial. Sometimes, in an even more microscopic way, we simply individuate particular duties and rights, depending on the current focus of attention. But this "static" conception proves to be misnamed; it concerns not stasis, but rather momentary normative judgement, whether the judgement envisaged is that of a court seeking to determine a litigated question, or that of a citizen engaged in practical judgement what to or demand in a given setting, or indeed that of a scholar trying to produce a coherent representation of some branch of the law. The recognition of rights and duties in this practical-judgemental setting is in any event an intellectual procedure different from that of seeking guidance about the valid exercise of normative power within a normative order dynamically conceived; the two interact and overlap, but are not the same. Law as normative order simply has two aspects, the dynamic and the momentary. Attempts like that of H. L. A. Hart to draw them together into a single structure of "primary and secondary rules" do not work, despite much ingenuity expended in trying to restate his view as a coherent whole.

IV. Conclusion

I have tried to show in outline how to approach an understanding of law as institutional normative order conceptually distinct from morality and from politics. By focusing on an idea of institutional normative order, one negates the existence of any analytically necessary nexus between law and state. Law is institutional normative order, and state-law is simply one form of law. Conversely, the state is a form of territorial political order with some internal power-structure and power-relations, and the law-state is simply one form of state. This entails a firm denial of Kelsen's assertion that every state is a *Rechtsstaat,* a law-state, on the ground that law and state are in effect the same object viewed in different terms.

They are not the same object at all. The law-state is in fact the only morally acceptable form of state, and the mere existence of some institutional normative order within a state does not guarantee that the state's power is effectively limited and regulated by law. That is a difficult but vitally important achievement of statecraft.

All this helps in building an understanding of the coming world order beyond the sovereign state. That order will enhance the moral significance of the law-state by enlarging and internationalising the legal order to which the state comes to be subjected. The development of a legal order under the European Human Rights Convention as well as the development of the legal order of the European Communities, and the subjection of European States ever more firmly to one, and in some cases to both, show the way forward here.

It always remains in the end a question whether the law constituted by some institutional normative order really has validity, really is binding. This can be handled in two ways. As a question of law, it receives a clear, but clearly self-referential answer. Any purported legal provision is either a valid member of a given system or not, either binding according to that system or not. But the law itself through those it determines to be competent judges regulates the answer to the question posed. Such answers have the merit of being objective, often clear, and authoritative.

The interpersonal objectivity of such judgements is a great merit in them, both from a prudential and from a moral point of view. But from the standpoint of the autonomous judgement, the price of interpersonal objectivity is, as always, heteronomy. If it is right to insist on the judgement of the autonomous moral agent as the final touchstone of morality, two things follow: even the most morally acceptable form of law remains crucially distinct from morality itself; and the ultimate basis of normative practical judgement ought to be morality, not law. The binding force of law is either a simple matter of intra-systemic, self-referential, and self-authenticating judgement, or it is for some moral agent autonomously endorsed. Only in the latter case is it fully normative. Only then does it, or should it, guide conduct categorically.

RECHTSTHEORIE 28 (1997), S. 235 - 242
Duncker & Humblot, 12165 Berlin

LEGAL SCIENCE AND ITS INFLUENCE ON JURISDICTION

By Agustín Squella, Valparaiso

I.

As is well known, Otto Brusiin created the basis for the future and the productive development of legal philosophy in Finland after World War II. I believe his work has been productive because it has, above all, been a legal philosophy created by and for jurists, not the mere abstractions disconnected from juridical experience that are usually pursued by those that Ihering ironically called the inhabitants of the "heaven of juridical concepts". As Aulis Aarnio has stated, "Otto Brusiin was the persistent explorer, seer and educator in Finnish legal culture". And though it is true that Otto Brusiin "cannot be directly associated with the tradition of analytical legal theory", it is nevertheless true that he played an important role as a "background inspirator" of that orientation in the juridical thinking of his country.

These are not mere pleasantries. The reading I have made of the two works of Brusiin translated into Spanish – *The Objectivity of Jurisdiction* and *Juridical Thought* – has been quite an adventure. For me, it has had all the elements always present in adventures: interest, excitement and discovery. Both works are certainly ambitious, particularly the latter, for Brusiin adopts two different viewpoints in his analysis of the juridical world without confusing them. First we find him going through the traditional course of legal theory or legal dogmatics, adopting later the sociological, historical and anthropological point of view. But although both works are ambitious, they are also extremely lucid and clarifying, particularly in connection to the activity of the judge in which Brusiin acknowledges the concurrence of cognitive and evaluative elements.

It is also worth noting the way in which Brusiin enters into an ongoing and accomplished dialogue with European thinkers of such distinctive characteristics as Max Weber, Hans Kelsen, Eugen Ehrlich, Rudolf Stammler, Karl Engisch, Francesco Carnelutti, Norberto Bobbio, Alf Ross and Georg Henrik von Wright. It is encouraging for a Latin American reader to realise that Brusiin's dialogue is also extended to Spanish-speaking authors such as Xabier Zubiri, Jose Ortega y Gasset,

Luis Legaz Lacambra and Carlos Cossio, whom he seems to know very well.

Lastly, and before getting into our subject of interest, I wish to emphasise the continuous concern that Brusiin displays for the urgency to obtain a certain rationality both in the theoretical and the practical activities of the jurist and in the activities of the judge. It is true that we cannot expect much in this respect. Man continues to threaten his own earthly existence and seems unable to find a way out, or rather finds it when it is already too late. Fortunately, it is not too late yet. And we have the words of Pascal, admired by Brusiin: "L'homme n'est qu'un roseau, le plus faible de la nature, mais c'est un roseau pensant."

II.

I wish to deal with both the way in which legal science – or legal dogmatics – projects itself onto jurisdiction and how it influences it. I believe that we can find a good starting point by establishing the meaning of legal dogmatics and jurisdiction from the first pages of one of Brusiin's works where he also conceptualises his understanding of "law". According to Brusiin, we may define "law" as an array of norms that is an enacted legal order partially created through specialised organisations of the community. This conceptualisation acknowledges, of course, that law is not only created by the organisations or the authorities of the community. It is also – to a great extent – created by the people themselves: They create law through juridical customs and contracts.

"Law" and "legal order" are, consequently, synonyms in the common language of jurists. It is necessary, nevertheless, to distinguish between "legal order" and "legal system". The first, as we have already stated, is law, whereas the latter represents a construction carried out by the science of law. I repeat that I find these ideas of Brusiin a good starting point in understanding law, legal science or dogmatics, jurisdiction, and, finally, the influence of legal science on jurisdiction.

If we scientifically understood law as an array of norms, that is, as a "legal order", what is first observed as self-evident is the set of rules. This means, above all, that law manifests itself as a given legal order in a given historical community at a given moment. It is also possible to think that law is comprised of legal norms, that is, law can also be defined as a specific norm for the regulation of human behaviour. It may also be conceivable that law does not, actually, consist of juridical norms, that juridical norms are but one among many of the elements structuring law. According to this point of view, law would not be essentially normative but a much more complex object in which it would be possible to identify both factual and evaluative elements. It is even possible to argue that law is not normative at all but, rather, "behaviour in intersubjective relations" and, consequently, juridical norms would only be a means to describe the reality of the specific behaviour of law. Lastly, some believe that juridical norms are not the law but only one of the elements used by judges in the creation of law.

These are, in that order, the points of view on law by authors such as Hans Kelsen, Miguel Reade (???), Carlos Cossio and Jerome Frank.

Regardless of whether one believes that juridical norms are the law, an element of law, a means to describe law, or just a simple element used by the judges to create true law, the truth is that juridical norms exist as such, that is, that there is something that we identify and call "juridical norms", and that, consequently, it is possible for juridical norms to become an object of knowledge. One of the various forms of knowledge of the juridical norms that constitute a given legal order is legal dogmatics. For this reason, legal dogmatics is a normative science, not because it prescribes or establishes norms, but because it deals with norms.

The scientific status of legal dogmatics can be argued about – this is a long and persistent debate within the history of juridical thought –, but what cannot be denied is its practical value. Or, to state it in another way, "knowledge does not have to be scientific in order to be useful and important". Brusiin advocates two reasons for calling this form of knowledge legal science. Firstly, he states that "we follow a traditional id... (???) use", and continues that if jurisprudence is acknowledged as science, particularly in its task of interpreting the law, then it is necessary to demand from jurisprudence what is expected of all sciences: objectivity. On the other hand, if jurisprudence is a "practical science" – as Brusiin strongly believes – it is not possible to demand that jurisprudence employs a "correct" method in its work; only a "fruitful" method is required. Obviously, Brusiin's idea is closely related to what was mentioned only a moment ago, that is, that knowledge does not need to be scientific in order to be significant.

Once it is established that the juridical norms of a given legal order constitute the object of legal dogmatics, we can see the operations performed by legal dogmatics in relation to its object of study.

a) Firstly, legal dogmatics locates or identifies the juridical norms of a given legal order.

b) Secondly, legal dogmatics resolves the possible meaning – or meanings – of juridical norms, which presupposes a task of interpretation.

c) Thirdly, legal dogmatics constructs a system of premises on juridical norms. For this reason, Otto Brusiin has written that "legal science is the interpretation of the law performed systematically". And he further adds that "a considerable part of the work done by jurists consists of the didactic presentation of the content of valid juridical norms".

d) Lastly, legal dogmatics provides an answer to practical problems that have arisen as a consequence of applying juridical norms to cases in societal life as they are debated before the courts of justice.

Legal dogmatics is, then, a "practical science". Using the words of Tercio Sampaio Ferraz, this means that "the statements that legal dogmatics makes can always be applied in coming to a decision". And Hernandez Gil further adds: "Legal dogmatics is, or purports to be, a science". The application of law, particularly juridical application, is a technique, an activity aimed at the solution of conflicts, but legal dogmatics is a theory concerned with the foundation and criticism of juridical decisions. Or, as Luhmann has stated, legal dogmatics "must not serve itself, but the application of law".

Regardless of whether legal dogmatics is mentioned in the positive legal order or not, it "exerts – as Brusiin says – an influence on jurisdiction", that is, on the activity of the judge. And Brusiin will further add that "the ever increasing importance of the position of legal science in the practice of law is an outcome of the general trend towards rationalisation in modern states". And still further: for the judges, legal science does not only furnish an external support "but has become an organic part of their way of thinking, of their personality as a whole".

This means that the judge is not a scientist prompted by theoretical goals; he is an authority and, as such, makes decisions that produce juridical norms for the solution of real cases in societal life, not hypotheses or laboratory experiments. Nevertheless, research in legal science, the outcome of scientific – or at least rigorous – knowledge concerning a specific legal order, has a strong influence on the choice of the possible solutions reached by the judge. Furthermore, this research – at least in the case of the more cultivated and learned judges – is incorporated into the judge's way of thinking in coming to his decisions. It is, of course, not the only element that influences the decisions of the judge, but its importance cannot, and must not, be dismissed, particularly if it is desirable that the theoretical work of jurists is to have a practical projection, a real presence in the life of law.

On the other hand, juridical decisions themselves, that is, the outcome of jurisdictional activity, are, in turn, brought forward, collected, systematised and disseminated by legal science, a fact that reinforces the stability of the decisions themselves, thus configurating a sort of circuit between legal science and jurisdiction.

Referring to Roman jurists, Savigny clearly stated that theory and practice cannot be set apart because "theory perfects itself through its more immediate application, and practice is ennobled by scientific treatment". For the same reason, Brusiin is right in apprising that theory and practice "should not follow different ways". "On the contrary, there will always be reciprocal movement between them representing a benefit for juridical culture". As Aarnio has stated: "The considerations that are (or may be) regarded as purely theoretical are, in fact, an *essential* part in any legal research that claims to be first and foremost practical".

And Ihering, Savigny's rebellious disciple, could point out that "to write on law deliberately overlooking the practical applicability of the matter is like making a clock taking great pains with its ornamentation and no care whatsoever with its mechanism". The practical value of legal dogmatics can be appreciated by noting – as Manuel Atienza (?) does – that "a legal order lacking dogmatic elaboration would be in a situation where fewer problems are solved than in the same legal order provided with adequate legal dogmatics".

III.

Our analysis so far will enable us to say that what is called "legal dogmatics" does not only have a cognitive function – it identifies and describes a specific legal order – but a political function, as well, manifest in the various effects its conclusions may have on societal life. The theoretical discourse of jurists certainly exerts its influence on the professional formation of future judges and legislators and, even more directly, on the productive work of judges and legislators. Juridical science is always interested – consciously or not – in the preservation or the change of the legal order to which its proportions or statements refer to.

The statements through which legal science describes its object, that is, the juridical norms of a given legal order, are never completely limited to description; usually they expand into criticism of the very same norms, that is, into approval if they are deemed convenient or socially useful, or into disapproval if they are regarded as inconvenient or socially undesirable.

Legal science always goes hand in hand with legal policy, although moments of description and criticism often appear to be methodologically apart. If in "description" the preservation of a given law seems to be favoured, in "criticism", on the other hand, it is quite possible to exert an influence on the judges and legislators in one way or the other: to either preserve or to change the law.

It is true – as Brusiin says – that legal science must be objective in the sense of adhering to what is given as law. But the objectivity of legal science is never unconditional, because the description of what is given as law may be biased by the interests and the prejudices of the jurist performing the description. Even if this is not the case and the jurist conducts his work in a perfectly impartial way, any description of law is inevitably followed by some apparent consequences relating to legal policy.

IV.

Jurisdiction must also be objective – so Brusiin assumes – because, in his work, the judge must proceed according to given juridical norms. These juridical norms have previously evaluated juridical situations in a specific way, and the judge must now identify this evaluation and come to a decision accordingly. Although the judge creates law, he is, nevertheless, subordinate to a higher power just as the legislature, a creator of law as well, is an organisation subordinate in relation to the Constitution. But the judge does not limit his activities to the "application of ready-made juridical norms to concrete cases".

We are now coming to the end of this brief review, and it is necessary to remind ourselves that although Otto Brusiin believes in the objectivity of jurisdiction, this can only be established through conformity by the judge to the law established prior to the cases in which he must intervene. This claim, however, requires a brief look at Brusiin's concepts of "jurisdiction" and "the objectivity principle".

Brusiin, in fact, understands jurisdiction as the agency of decision-making entrusted to certain communal authorities – the judge – through "procedural" norms. The function of these authorities is the application of abstract norms in evaluating and deciding concrete situations. Brusiin's objectivity principle of jurisdiction, on the other hand, reads as follows: "This principle means that the judges must guide their conduct, and particularly their decisions, according to the juridical norms that regulate the very same conduct and decisions." (???)

Brusiin further states that although jurisdiction must be objective, this is never accomplished in full. It is adequate that jurisprudence is objective to a "high degree", for there will always be non-objective cases as in, for instance, political processes. This does not, however, imply that jurisdiction, considered as a whole, may be defined as non-objective. Brusiin then inquires into the facts that support the objectivity of jurisdiction. In identifying these elements, Brusiin not only mentions juridical norms regulating the activity of the judge, but includes his education, legal science, the theory of interpreting the law, and what he calls the "social control of the members of the community". The elements that support objectivity are of a very difficult nature. On the one hand, they may reinforce one another, that is, aim toward similar goals, but this is not necessarily the case. They may also collide and place the judge in an extremely difficult position, a dilemma that Alf Ross describes well by distinguishing between the formal juridical conscience and the material juridical conscience of the judge.

V.

The objectivity of the jurist's work in describing the law as it is and not as it should be according to a personal point of view can never become an obstacle that would impede him from having or expressing opinions of a political or moral nature. The jurist must pay attention simultaneously to his duty as a scientist and to his political and moral conscience. He must not sacrifice his scientific vocation to his political convictions, for this would impoverish his understanding of reality. But neither can he appeal to science in order to evade positions in the political field, for in this case he might risk being diminished as a human being and a citizen.

A judge must also be objective and, furthermore, it is necessary that his activities be executed in a non-arbitrary way but bound to pre-established juridical norms. But objectivity does not free the judge from his duty to fairness, nor does it liberate him from responsibility for the decisions taken. A judge whose behaviour is not objective is, of course, a threat to his fellowmen. But a judge that obeys the law in all cases, even when its application would lead to consequences that are clearly unfair or improper, will fail to satisfy the legal demand for justice that is present in every individual that appeals to the courts.

If the task of a judge is not easy, to be a good judge is even harder. A judge must be objective. A good judge must not only be objective. Brusiin has accurately pointed out that there are different elements supporting or aiding the judge in his quest for objectivity. But Brusiin's greatest achievement is, perhaps, to have shown that the objectivity of a judge is not equivalent to blind submission to the law but to its rational application. In other words, even when the judge speaks the law, he is not only a channel through which the voice of the legislator can be heard. The legal system is, then, not a system of fully determined prescriptions, nor is it true that there is a single correct legal solution to every juridical case.

The judge is certainly not a legislator, but neither is he merely the voice of the legislator.

RECHTSTHEORIE 28 (1997), S. 243 - 250
Duncker & Humblot, 12165 Berlin

BIBLIOGRAPHY OTTO BRUSIIN

A. List of the Legal-Theoretical Works of Otto Brusiin

I. Monographs

1. Tuomarin harkinta normin puuttuessa (Das richterliche Ermessen in Lückenfällen), Diss. (Helsinki), Vammala 1938, XXI, 267pp. (Deutsche Zusammenfassung), Publikationen des Finnischen Juristenvereins Nr. 14.

2. Über die Objektivität der Rechtsprechung, Helsinki 1949, 122pp.

   Spanish translation: La objetivitad de la jurisdicción, translated by Ernesto Garzón Valdés, Córdoba/Argentinien 1966.

3. Über das juristische Denken, Helsinki 1951, 164pp., Societas Scientiarum Fennica, Commentationes Humanarum Litterarum, XVII, 5.

   Spanish translation: El pensamiento jurídico, translated by José Puig Brutau, Buenos Aires 1959, Ediciones Jurídicas Europa-América, Breviarios de derecho 18.

4. Aineettoman vahingon korvaamisesta. Siviilioikeudellinen tutkimus (Über den Ersatz des immateriellen Schadens nach finnischem Zivilrecht), Helsinki 1953, 182pp.

5. Zum Ehescheidungsproblem. Eine rechtstheoretische Studie, Hyvinkää 1959, 134pp.

6. Zum Problem des immateriellen Schadens, Turku 1966, 81pp. (Annales Universitatis Turkuensis, ser. B, tom. 96).

7. Wexionius-Studien I. Grundsätzliches zur Rechtswissenschaft, Turku 1968, 36pp. (Annales Universitatis Turkuensis, ser. B, tom. 109).

8. Bilmark-Studien I. Einführung in das Studium der Philosophie Johan Bilmarks, Turku 1971, 33pp. (Annales Universitatis Turkuensis, ser. B, tom. 120).

9. Wexionius-Studien II. Fasciculuc Juridicus, Turku 1971, 37pp. (Annales Universitatis Turkuensis, ser. B, tom. 121).

10. Bilmark-Studien II. De matrimonio conscientiae, Turku 1972, 31pp. (Annales Universitatis Turkuensis, ser. B, tom. 124).

II. Essays

11. Tieteellisestä ajattelusta (Über das wissenschaftliche Denken), in: Valvoja-Aika 12 (1934), pp. 20 - 34.

12. Oikeusfilosofia ja käytäntö (Rechtsphilosophie und das praktische Rechtsleben), in: Defensor Legis 15 (1934), pp. 243 - 254.

13. Oikeellisuudesta (Über die Gerechtigkeit), in: Defensor Legis 16 (1935), pp. 31 - 46.

14. Joustavat normit oikeudenkäytössä (Die Anwendung der elastischen Normen), in: Defensor Legis 19 (1938), pp. 286 - 293.

15. Den nya italienska civilrätten (Das neue italienische Zivilgesetzbuch), in: Tidskrift, utgiven av Juridiska Föreningen i Finland 79 (1943), pp. 27 - 43.

16. Gustav II Adolfs krigsartiklar. Några synpunkter (Die Kriegsartikel von Gustav II Adolf. Einige Gesichtspunkte), in: Tidskrift, utgiven av Juridiska Föreningen i Finland 79 (1943), pp. 373 - 393.

17. Oikeudellisesta ajattelusta (Über das rechtliche Denken), in: Valvoja 22 (1944), pp. 133 - 140.

18. Oikeustiede ja käytäntö (Rechtswissenschaft und Rechtspraxis), in: Defensor Legis 25 (1944), pp. 197 - 204.

19. Oikeusteoriasta (Über die Rechtstheorie), in: Valtiotieteellisen yhdistyksen vuosikirja 7 (1947), pp. 22 - 28.

20. Om allmän rättsteori (Über die allgemeine Rechtstheorie), in: Nya argus 43 (1950), pp. 272f.

21. Über die finnische Rechtsphilosophie, Brüssel 1950, 9 pp., Meddelingen van de Koninklikje vlaamse academie woor wetenschappen, letteren en schone kunsten van Belgie, Klasse de letteren 12:8.

22. Das Deduktive im juristischen Denken, in: ARSP 39 (1950/51), pp. 324 - 337.

23. Antiikin ihmisen ymmärtämisestä (Über das Verständnis des Menschen der Antike), in: Ajatus (Jahrbuch der finnischen philosophischen Vereinigung) 17 (1952), pp. 38 - 47.

24. Carlos Cossio, in: Finsk Tidskrift 152 (1952), pp. 182 - 187.

25. Piirteitä Vilhelm Lundstedtin ajatusmaailmasta (Das Denken Vilhelm Lundstedts – einige Aspekte), in: Lakimies 50 (1952), pp. 559 - 564.

26. La apreciación judicial en casos de lagunas, in: Revista facultad de derecho – Tucuman/Argentinien 10 (1954), pp. 105 - 116.

27. Oikeusvertailusta (Über die Rechtsvergleichung), in: Lakimies 52 (1954), pp. 559 - 564.

28. Legal Theory. Some Considerations, in: ARSP 43 (1957), pp. 465 - 469.

29. International Aspects of Legal Theory, in: Estudios jurídico-sociales homenaje al profesor Luis Legaz y Lacambra I, 1960, pp. 245 - 250.

30. Methodological Aspects of Legal Theory, in: Studi in onore di Emilio Betti I, 1960, pp. 41 - 48.

31. Zum 50jährigen Bestehen der Internationalen Vereinigung für Rechts- und Sozialphilosophie, in: ARSP, Beiheft 38 (1960), pp. 1 - 14.

32. Erzieherische Ausblicke der rechtswissenschaftlichen Grundlagenforschung, in: ARSP 47 (1961), pp. 387 - 393.

33. Roomalaisesta oikeudesta (Über das römische Recht), in: Lakimies 59 (1961), pp. 239 - 252.

34. Yleisestä oikeusteoriasta (Über die allgemeine Rechtstheorie), in: Suomalainen Suomi 1962, pp. 159 - 163.

35. Zur Ideengeschichte der Rechtstheorie, in: Jahrbuch für Internationales Recht 11 (1962), pp. 19 - 24.

36. Aspects philosophiques du droit romain, in: Mélanges en l'honneur de Jean Dabin, 1963, pp. 27 - 31.

37. Müßige Fragen der Naturrechtsphilosophie, in: Legal Essays – Festskrift til Frede Castberg, 1963, pp. 64 - 73.

38. Reine Rechtslehre und Rechtsvergleichung, in: ARSP 49 (1963), pp. 319 - 322.

39. Prosessiteoriaa 1600-luvun Turussa (Prozeßtheorie in Turku im 17. Jahrhundert), in: Lakimies 62 (1964), pp. 709 - 719.

40. Rechtsvergleichung in Finnland im 17. Jahrhundert, in: Ius Privatum Gentium. Festschrift für Max Rheinstein zum 70. Geburtstag am 5. Juli 1969, 1. Rechtsmethodik und internationales Recht, ed. by Ernst von Cammerer, Soia Mentschikoff and Konrad Zweigert, Tübingen 1969, pp. 235 - 245.

41. Professor Fahlander och mångiftet, in: Nordisk gjenklang. Festskrift til Carl Jacob Arnholm 18, desember 1969, Oslo 1969, pp. 683 - 692.

42. Zur Idee der Disputation, in: Studia philosophica in honorem Sven Krohn septuagesimum annum complentis 9.V.1973, Turku 1973, pp. 37 - 44. (Annales Universitatis Turkuensis, ser. B, tom. 126).

43. Legal philosophy in 17th century Finland: some reflections, in: Scandinavian studies in law, Uppsala 18 (1974), pp. 11 - 25.

44. Scienza universale, in: Inchieste di diritto comparatto, 2., Italy 1973, pp. 41 - 54.

III. Reviews

45. Brynolf *Hohkasalo*, Kausaalisuuskysymys rikosoikeudessa, in: Valvoja-Aika 11 (1933), pp. 520 - 522.

46. Hans *Fehr*, Oikeus ja todellisuus (übersetzt von Alli Haataja), in: Valvoja-Aika 11 (1933), pp. 522 - 524.

47. Arvo *Sipilä*, Deliktiperusteisen vahingonvastuun teoreettinen rakenne Suomen varallisuusoikeutta silmällä pitäen, in: Valvoja-Aika 15 (1937), pp. 327 - 337.

48. S. R. *Björksten*, Kansainvälinen oikeus, in: Valvoja-Aika 15 (1937), pp. 425f.

49. Robert S. *Woodworth*, Psykologia, in: Lakimies 1938, p. 407.

50. Nils *Herlitz*, Svensk frihet, in: Tidskrift, utgiven av Juridiska Föreningen i Finland 79 (1943), pp. 407f.

51. Fr. *Kruse-Vinding*, Retslaeren I - II; *idem*, Erkendelse og Vurdering, in: Tidskrift, utgiven av Juridiska Föreningen i Finland 80 (1944), pp. 138 - 141.

52. Erik *Ahlman*, Oikeudenmukaisuus ja sen suhde moraaliin, in: Tidskrift, utgiven av Juridiska Föreningen i Finland 80 (1944), pp. 141f.

53. R. A. *Wrede*, Suomen oikeus - ja yhteiskuntajärjestys, in: Lakimies 1945, pp. 551f.

54. Veli *Merikoski*, Suomen julkisoikeuden oppikirja I - II, in: Lakimies 1946, pp. 420 - 422.

55. Giorgio *Del Vecchio*, Lezioni di filosofia del diritto, in: Lakimies 1947, p. 128.

56. Francesco *Messineo*, Manuale di diritto civile e commerciale I - II, in: Lakimies 1947, pp. 128f.

57. Adolf F. *Schnitzler*, Vergleichende Rechtslehre, in: Lakimies 1947, pp. 163 - 165.

58. Hans *Kelsen*, General Theory of Law and State, in: Lakimies 1947, p. 542.

59. Matthias *Calonius*, Siviilioikeuden luennot, in: Valvoja-Aika 25 (1947), p. 91.

60. Guido *Calogero*, Etica. Giuridica. Politica, in: Valvoja-Aika 25 (1947), p. 91.

61. Aatos *Alanen*, Yleinen oikeustiede, in: Lakimies 1949, pp. 75 - 77.

62. Wilhelm R. *Beyer*, Rechtsphilosophische Gesinnung, in: Lakimies 1949, p. 81.

63. A. I. *Denisov*, Valtio - ja oikeusteoria, in: Lakimies 1949, p. 600.

64. J. N. *Lehtinen*, Mitä oikeus on?, in: Defensor Legis 1949, pp. 398 - 401.

65. Francesco *Calasso*, Introduzione al diritto comune; *idem*, I glossatori e la teoria della sovranità, in: Tidskrift, utgiven av Juridiska Föreningen i Finland 1950, pp. 240f.

66. Alessandro *Levi*, Teoria generale del diritto, in: Tidskrift, utgiven av Juridiska Föreningen i Finland 1950, pp. 296f.

67. Commentario sistematico alla costituzione italiana I - II, in: Tidskrift, utgiven av Juridiska Föreningen i Finland 1950, pp. 297f.

68. Emilio *Betti*, Interpretazione delle legge e degli atti giuridici, in: Tidskrift, utgiven av Juridiska Föreningen i Finland 1950, pp. 298f.

69. Pietro *Piovani*, Normatività e società, in: Tidskrift, utgiven av Juridiska Föreningen i Finland 1950, p. 299.

70. Wilhelm *Sauer*, Grundlagen der Wissenschaft und der Wissenschaften; *idem*, System der Rechts- und Sozialphilosophie; *idem*, Völkerrecht und Weltfrieden; *idem*, Allgemeine Strafrechtslehre, Festschrift für Wilhelm Sauer, in: Tidskrift, utgiven av Juridiska Föreningen i Finland 1950, pp. 299 - 301.

71. Jan Magnus *Jansson*, Hans Kelsens statsteori mot bakgrunden av hans rättsfilosofiska åskådning, in: ARSP 39 (1950/51), pp. 577 - 579 and Defensor Legis 1951, pp. 308 - 309.

72. Ch. *Boasson*, Sociological Aspects of Law and International Adjustment, in: Nordisk Tidsskrift for Internationel Ret og Jus Gentium 1951, pp. 139f.

73. Mario *Giuliano*, La comunità internazionale e il diritto, in: Nordisk Tidsskrift for Internationel Ret og Jus Gentium 1951, pp. 138f.

74. Francesco Elias *De Tejada*, Las doctrinas políticas en la Cataluña medieval, in: Tidskrift, utgiven av Juridiska Föreningen i Finland 1951, pp. 239f.

75. J. *Haesart*, Préalables du droit international public; *idem*, Les prétendus principes généraux de la politique international et du droit de gens; *idem*, Obstacles à la cohesion de l'Europe, in: Tidskrift, utgiven av Juridiska Föreningen i Finland 1951, pp. 241f.

76. Francesco *Carnelutti*, Teoria generale del diritto, in: Tidskrift, utgiven av Juridiska Föreningen i Finland 1951, pp. 242f.

77. Veikko *Reinikainen*, Suomen lainopillinen kirjallisuus 1809 - 1948, in: Finsk Tidskrift 1951, pp. 45f.

78. *Kelsen*, *Cossio*, Problemas escogidos de la teoría pura del derecho, in: Tidskrift for Retsvitenskap 1952, pp. 462 - 468.

79. Enrique R. *Aftalión*, Critica del saber de los juristas, in: Tidskrift for Retsvitenskap 1952, pp. 468 - 472.

80. Luigi *Bagolini*, Valutazioni morali e giuridiche nella crisi dell' etica individuale, in: Tidskrift for Retsvitenskap 1953, pp. 554 - 556.

81. O. Hj. *Granfelt*, Friherre Rabbe Axel Wrede. Universitetslärare och vetenskapsman. Domare. Adademiekansler, in: Nya argus 1952, pp. 21f.

82. Eberhard *Schmidt*, Gesetz und Richter, in: Lakimies 1953, pp. 608f.

83. Frede *Castberg*, Fra statslivets retsproblemer, in: Lakimies 1954, p. 401.

84. Francesco *Calasso*, Introduzione al diritto comune, in: Lakimies 1954, pp. 402 - 404.

85. Paul *Koschaker*, Europa und das römische Recht, in: Lakimies 1954, pp. 402f.

86. Vilhelm *Aubert*, Torstein *Eckhoff*, Knut *Sveri*, En lov i søkelyset, in: ARSP 41 (1955)b, pp. 453 - 456.

87. B. C. *Carlson*, Rätten. Ett rättsteoretiskt försök, in: ARSP 41 (1954/55), pp. 450 - 452.

88. Hans *Kelsen*, Théorie pure du droit, in: Tidskrift, utgiven av Juridiska Föreningen i Finland 1956, p. 172.

89. Edwin W. *Patterson*, Jurisprudence, in: Tidskrift, utgiven av Juridiska Föreningen i Finland 1956, pp. 172f.

90. Norberto *Bobbio*, Studi sulla teoria generale del diritto, in: Tidskrift, utgiven av Juridiska Föreningen i Finland 1956, pp. 173f.

91. Uberto *Scarpelli*, Filosofia analitica e giurisprudenza; *idem*, Il problema della definizione e il concetto di diritto, in: Tidskrift, utgiven av Juridiska Föreningen i Finland 1956, pp. 173f.

92. Josef *Esser*, Grundsatz und Norm in der richterlichen Fortbildung des Privatrechts, in: ARSP 43 (1957), pp. 460 - 464.

93. Fritz *von Hippel*, Zum Aufbau und Sinneswandel unseres Privatrechts, in: ARSP 44 (1958), p. 135f.

94. Alessandro *Levi*, Scritti minori, in: ARSP 44 (1958), pp. 572 - 574.

95. Pietro *Piovani*, Linee di una filosofia del diritto, in: ARSP 45 (1959), pp. 214f.

96. Walter G. *Becker*, Gegenopfer und Opferverwehrung, in: Lakimies 1959, p. 97.

97. Rapports relatifs à la Finlande préséntés au V Congrès international de droit comparé, in: Lakimies 1959, pp. 91 - 98.

98. Scandinavian Studies in Law, in: Lakimies 1959, pp. 181f.

99. Werner *Goldschmidt*, La Ciencia de la Justicia, in: Tidskrift for Retsvitenskap 1960, pp. 255 - 257.

100. Cesare *Magni*, Avviamento allo studio analitico del diritto ecclesiastico; *ders.*, Interpretazione del diritto italiano sulle credenze di religione. I. Possibilità operative analitice e structure d'ordine delle scelte normative, in: Tidskrift for Retsvitenskap 1960, pp. 501f.

101. *Wolf, Lüke, Hax*, Scheidung und Scheidungsrecht, in: Ehe und Familie 1960, pp. 38 - 40.

102. Sten *Gagnér*, Studien zur Ideengeschichte der Gesetzgebung, in: Tidskrift, utgiven av Juridiska Föreningen i Finland 1961, pp. 262f.

103. J. Gillis *Wetter*, The Styles of Appellate Judicial Opinions. A Case Study in Comparative Law, in: Tidskrift, utgiven av Juridiska Föreningen i Finland 1961, pp. 352f.

104. R. B. *Schlesinger*, Comparative Law. Cases, Text, Materials, in: Tidskrift, utgiven av Juridiska Föreningen i Finland 1961, p. 353.

105. Mario *Rotondi*, Studi di diritto commerciale e di diritto generale delle obbligazioni, in: Tidskrift, utgiven av Juridiska Föreningen i Finland 1961, pp. 353f.

106. Karl *Larenz*, Methodenlehre der Rechtswissenschaft, in: Tidskrift for Retsvitenskap 1961, pp. 618 - 621.

107. Werner *Goldschmidt*, Introducción al Derecho. Estructura del mundo jurídico, in: ARSP 50 (1964), pp. 141 - 144.

108. Kaarle *Makkonen*, Zur Problematik der juridischen Entscheidung. Eine strukturanalytische Studie, in: Lakimies 1965, pp. 927 - 930.

109. Frede *Castberg*, Forelesninger over rettsfilosofi, in: Tidskrift for Retsvitenskap 1966, pp. 254 - 256.

110. Max *Gutzwiller*, Elemente der Rechtsidee. Ausgewählte Aufsätze und Reden, in: Tidskrift for Retsvitenskap 1966, pp. 397f.

B. Reviews of the Works of Otto Brusiin

Tuomarin harkinta normin puuttuessa (1938)

1. *Carlson*, B. C., in: Defensor Legis 1938, pp. 316 - 328.

2. *Kaila*, Elieser, in: Lakimies 1938, pp. 385 - 408 and Nordisk Administrativ Tidskrift 1939, pp. 33 - 36.

3. *af Hällström*, Erik, in: Tidskrift, utgiven av Juridiska Föreningen i Finland 1939, pp. 568 - 570 and Svensk Juristtidning 24 (1939), pp. 764 - 766.

Über die Objektivität der Rechtsprechung (1949)

1. *Becker,* Walter G., in: Archiv für die Civilistische Praxis 1950/51, p. 367.
2. *Weigelen,* Ernst, in: ARSP 39 (1950), pp. 438 - 441.
3. *Sauer,* Wilhelm, in: Deutsche Rechts-Zeitschrift 5 (1950), p. 287.
4. *Lahtinen,* Osvi, in: Defensor Legis 1950, pp. 42 - 46.
5. *af Hällström,* Erik, in: Tidskrift, utgiven av Juridiska Föreningen i Finland 1950, pp. 305 f.
6. *Merkl,* Adolf, in: Juristische Blätter 72 (1950), pp. 514 f.
7. *Larenz,* Karl, in: Neue Juristische Wochenschrift 1 (1950), pp. 168 - 172.
8. *Minvervini,* G., in: Rassegna di diritto pubblico 1950, pp. 117 f.
9. *Carnelutti,* Francesco, in: Rivista di diritto processuale 1950, p. 181.
10. *Simson,* Gerhard, in: Svensk Juristtidning 35 (1950), pp. 284 - 286.
11. *Ross,* Alf, in: Tidskrift for Retsvitenskap 1950, pp. 473 - 478.
12. *Spanner,* H., in: Österreichische Zeitschrift für öffentliches Recht 3 (1950), pp. 604 - 606.
13. *Alanen,* Aatos, in: Lakimies 1951, pp. 360 - 362.
14. *de Tejada,* Francesco Elias, in: Revista general de legislación y jurisprudencia 1951, pp. 25 - 27.
15. *Cohn,* E. J., in: The modern law review 1952, p. 129.
16. *Wolffers,* A., in: Schweizerische Juristen-Zeitung 48 (1952), p. 115.
17. *Goldschmidt,* Werner, in: Revista del instituto de derecho civil (Tucuman) 1953, p. 104.

Über das juristische Denken (1951)

1. *Zimmermann,* Theo, in: ARSP 40 (1952/53), pp. 607 f.
2. *Van Schmid,* J. J., in: Rechtskundig Weekblad 1952, p. 143.
3. *Gregoire,* V., in: Revue des sciences philosophiques et théologiques 1952, pp. 681 f.
4. *Carnelutti,* Francesco, in: Rivista di diritto processuale 7 (1952), pp. 5 f.
5. *Spanner,* H., in: Österreichische Zeitschrift für öffentliches Recht 4 (1952), pp. 559 f.
6. *Lehtinen,* J. N., in: Lakimies 1953, pp. 787 - 789.
7. *Goldschmidt,* Werner, in: Revista del instituto de derecho civil 1953, pp. 129 - 131.
8. *Meier-Hayoz,* Arthur, in: Schweizerische Juristenzeitung 49 (1953), p. 68.
9. *Cohn,* E. J., in: The modern law review 1953, pp. 125 f.
10. *Ehrenzweig,* Albert, in: Österreichische Juristen-Zeitung 8 (1953), pp. 110 f.
11. *Tammelo,* Ilmar, in: The American Journal of Comparative Law 3 (1954), pp. 292 f.
12. *Mokre,* Johann, in: Juristische Blätter 77 (1955), p. 612.

13. *Palazzolo,* Vincenzo, in: Rivista internazionale di filosofia del diritto 33 (1956), pp. 688 - 690.

14. *Orfield,* Lester B., in: Wisconsin Law Review 1956, pp. 474 - 477.

15. *von Kempski,* Jürgen, in: Zeitschrift für die gesamte Staatswissenschaft 113 (1957), pp. 566 - 571.

Aineettoman vahingon korvaamisesta (1953)

Rautiala, Martti, in: Lakimies 1955, pp. 590 - 592.

Zum Ehescheidungsproblem (1959)

1. *Arnholm,* Carl Jacob, in: Tidskrift for Retsvitenskap 1959, pp. 159 - 164.

2. *Makkonen,* Kaarle, in: Lakimies 1959, pp. 891 - 895.

3. *Unger,* J., in: The Modern Law Review 1959, pp. 571 - 573.

4. *Roggwiller,* Hans, in: Schweizerische Juristen-Zeitung 55 (1959), pp. 318 - 319.

5. *Persico,* Giovanni, in: Rivista trimestriale di diritto e procedura civile 1959, pp. 606 - 608.

6. *Bognette,* Giovanni, in: Rivista internazionale di filosofia del diritto 36 (1959), pp. 621 - 624.

7. *De Cupis,* Adriano, in: Diritto e giurisprudenza 1959.

8. *Becker,* Walter G., in: ARSP 46 (1960), pp. 448 - 452.

9. *Rheinstein,* Max, in: The American Journal of Comparative Law 1960, pp. 135 - 137.

10. *Lasok,* D., in: The International and Comparative Law Quarterly 9 (1960), pp. 158f.

11. *Merz,* Hans, in: Zeitschrift des Bernischen Juristenvereins 96 (1960), pp. 34f.

12. *Schwind,* Fritz, in: Ehe und Familie 1960, p. 172 and Österreichische Juristen-Zeitung 15 (1960).

13. *Pritsch,* Erich, in: Zeitschrift für vergleichende Rechtswissenschaft 63 (1961), pp. 262 - 267.

14. *Sachers,* Erich, in: Juristische Blätter 83 (1961), pp. 300f.

15. *Jülkenbeck,* Hermann, in: Kölner Zeitschrift für Soziologie und Sozialpsychologie 15 (1963), pp. 173f.

FSC
www.fsc.org
MIX
Papier aus verantwortungsvollen Quellen
Paper from responsible sources
FSC® C105338

Printed by Libri Plureos GmbH
in Hamburg, Germany